About the Author

Dean Spitzer, Ph.D., is a pioneer in the development of new approaches to improving the quality of education and training.

Spitzer has been a professor at four universities, including a visiting professorship in Australia (where he consulted with some of the largest companies in the country). He has been a senior trainer and training manager with two Fortune 500 corporations, the U.S. government, and the Kuwait government. He has consulted with more than fifty public and private organizations around the world.

This book is part of the *Techniques in Training and Performance Development Series*, developed and edited by Joseph W. Arwady, Corporate Director, Training and Performance Development, Baker Industries, division of Borg-Warner Corporation, Parsippany, New Jersey.

Improving Individual Performance

Techniques in
Training and Performance Development
Series

Improving Individual Performance

Dean R. Spitzer

Series Developer and Editor
Joseph W. Arwady

Educational Technology Publications
Englewood Cliffs, New Jersey 07632

Library of Congress Cataloging-in-Publication Data

Spitzer, Dean R.
  Improving individual performance.

  (Techniques in training and performance development series)
  Bibliography: p.
  Includes index.
  1. Employees, Training of. I. Title. II. Series.
HF5549.5.T7S655   1986   658.3'1243   86-8978
ISBN 0-87778-197-4

Copyright © 1986 Educational Technology Publications, Inc., Englewood Cliffs, New Jersey 07632.

All rights reserved. No part of this book may be reproduced or transmitted, in any form or by any means, electronic or mechanical, including photocopying, recording, or by any information storage and retrieval system, without permission in writing from the Publisher.

Printed in the United States of America.

Library of Congress Catalog Card Number: 86-8978.

International Standard Book Number: 0-87778-197-4.

First Printing: June, 1986.

FOR CYNTHIA, MY WIFE, MY HELPER,
MY COMPANION, MY BEST FRIEND

Acknowledgments

So many people have contributed to this book that it is difficult to know where to begin. So, let me begin here:
- Thanks to Joe Arwady for inviting me to contribute to this series and for his outstanding editorial suggestions and assistance.
- Thanks to Charles Ragland for his generous and invaluable counsel, his help in designing the figures, and his refreshing attitude toward learning and toward life.
- Thanks to Larry Lipsitz and Educational Technology Publications for their enlightened publications and courageous publishing policy.
- Thanks to Sivasailam "Thiagi" Thiagarajan and Harold Stolovitch, my mentors and friends.
- Thanks to the National Society for Performance and Instruction (NSPI) for providing me with a professional identity.
- Thanks to all the trainers who so generously shared "their" techniques with me.
- Thanks to all the organizations that enabled me to try out these techniques with their employees.
- Thanks to my parents and my step-parent for creating an optimal environment for my own learning, for their ceaseless encouragement, and (most of all) for their love.
- Thanks to God who gave me whatever ability I have and who provides me with whatever strength I muster to complete tasks such as this one. May it be to His glory.
- And last, but certainly not least, thanks to my wife Cynthia (to whom this book is dedicated) for her love, commitment, understanding, and total support of whatever (within reason) I decide to do.

Editor's Preface

"Prolific" is the word most often associated with Dean Spitzer. Although the count is not precise, Dean has authored over 100 publications. Not only does he write a good deal, but also he *says* a lot. Best of all, what he has to say is always practical; for some, painfully so. Not one to mince words or wander through already worn theory, Dean has a real-world view of training and performance development. He avoids unnecessary jargon and procedural formalities. His is not an attempt to be irreverent, only an honest interest in making a difference where it really counts—in the individual worker's capacity to approach optimal performance.

My first Spitzer reading was in 1978, just as I completed work on a Ph.D at Ohio State. Dean was a 1974 graduate of USC's doctoral program, and while I had aspirations of making a meaningful contribution to improving human performance, it was clear that Dean had already begun to make his. Over the years, I continued to be impressed by Dean's work and when the TECHNIQUES IN TRAINING AND PERFORMANCE DEVELOPMENT SERIES was only an idea brewing, Dean was one of the first people I contacted. At the time an internal management consultant at Kimberly-Clark Corp., he committed to the project immediately. I had a table of contents ten days later. He corresponded next from the Kuwait Institute for Scientific Research, where he had accepted a position as Training Advisor. Sending the introductory chapter, Dean resigned from the project, citing distance and new circumstances as reasons preventing him from meeting manuscript deadlines.

Dean was replaced with a suitable author and work on all ten books continued. Due to a series of untimely business conflicts, a second author was forced to resign from the project, leaving a collection of "manuscript starts" to show after twelve months of work. By now, the other books were well along the road to completion. I faced the prospect of finding a capable and respected replacement author on short notice. What to do?

The answer came during a conversation with a colleague in California, who mentioned that she had recently seen Dean Spitzer. I located him, learned that he had returned to the States permanently, and invited him to "re-author" a book in the series. For the second time, Dean accepted immediately. The timing was much better and a first draft of the *entire manuscript* arrived in *one month*. The rest is editing history as Dean and I exchanged drafts several times and delivered a final version of *Improving Individual Performance* to the publisher only six months after the originally scheduled delivery date.

I'm sure there's a moral here having something to do with "leaving the door open," "not counting your chickens until they hatch," or "good things coming to those who wait." Whatever the spiritual connotations, the practical significance for the reader is certain.

Improving Individual Performance bears the Spitzer trademark—clearly worded, well-organized, and oriented to the practitioner. Take advantage of Dean Spitzer's fifteen years as a training and performance analyst. Familiarize yourself, your staff, and your co-workers with each of his seventy-four techniques. Neophyte or mentor, this book contains the best kind of information and ideas—the kind you *use*, not simply read.

Joseph W. Arwady
Series Editor
February, 1986

Table of Contents

Acknowledgments.................................... vii

Editor's Preface..................................... ix

1. Introduction...................................... 3
   Why Working with Individuals?..................... 3
   What Does It Mean to Work with Individuals?....... 4
   What Is an Individual Training Technique?......... 5
   The Advantages of Working with Individuals........ 5
   The Importance of Individual Learning............. 6
   The Essentials of Learning........................ 6
   Preparing Learners for Learning 8
   Encouraging Appropriate Organizing of Information 8
   Providing Opportunities for Practicing Information Retrieval.. 9
   The Crucial Role of the Supervisor 10
   Organization of This Book 11
   How and Why the Techniques Were Selected 11
   My Responsibility and Your Responsibility 12
   Bibliography 13
   Final Admonitions 13

2. Preparing for Learning........................... 14
   Pre-Course Trainee-Supervisor Discussions Technique..... 14
   Pre-Course Trainee-Trainer Contacts Technique 16
   Training Needs Questionnaire Technique 18
   Preliminary Exercises Technique....................... 20
   Pre-Course Contract Technique......................... 22
   Supervisor Briefings Technique........................ 25
   Relaxation 1: Deep Breathing Technique 27
   Relaxation 2: Progressive Relaxation Technique........ 28

Acknowledging Feelings Technique. 30
Creative Name Tags Technique 31
Environmental Enrichment Technique 32
Personal Needs Analysis Technique. 33
Competency Visioning Technique. 36
Self-Affirmation Technique. 38
Overviewing Technique 40
Pre-Course Action Planning Technique 42
Personal Performance Analysis Technique. 44
Personal Objective Review Technique 46

3. Organizing Information. 49
Multi-Method Presentation Technique. 49
Mock Interview Technique 52
Drill Practice Technique 53
Humor Technique. 54
Question Recording Technique. 56
Personal Vantage Point Technique 58
Inviting Recall Technique 59
Key Concept Recording Technique. 60
Associative Thinking Technique 62
Concept Examples Technique. 63
Concept Diagramming Technique 65
Metaphor Technique. 67
Periodic Summarizing Technique 68
Concert Reading Technique 69
Repetition Technique 70
Fill in the Blanks Technique 71
Categorization of Notes Technique. 73
Objective Review Technique. 74
Glossary Development Technique. 75

4. Practice for Retrieval. 78
Multi-Phase Programming Technique. 78
Supervisor Meetings Technique. 80
Case Studies Technique. 82
Simulation Technique. 84
Note-Taking Technique. 85

Table of Contents

Individual Brainstorming Technique 86
Bumper Stickers Technique. 87
Developing Analogies Technique. 89
Objective Rewriting Technique 90
Shoulds, Wants, Wills Technique 91
Trainee Teaching Technique 94
Scavenger Hunt Technique 95
Personal Learning Journal Technique 96
Guided Imagery Technique. 98
Problem-Solving Technique. 100
Quality Dot Technique 101
Potential Problem Analysis Technique 103
Problems into Opportunities Technique 105
Video Feedback Technique. 107
Action Planning Technique. 108

5. Evaluation of Learning 111
Feedback Cards Technique 111
Flip-Chart Feedback Technique 113
Quizzing Technique. 114
Happiness Index Technique. 115
Trainee-Developed Evaluation Technique 117
Evaluation Indicator Identification Technique 118
Before and After Technique 120
Benefits and Costs Technique 122
Card Sorting Technique. 124
Trainee-Supervisor Evaluation Meeting Technique 126
Pre/Post Assessment Technique. 128
Delayed Questionnaire Technique. 129
Action Plan Follow-Up Technique 131
Evaluation Interview Technique 132
Critical Incident Evaluation Technique 134
Ask the Class Technique 136
Materials Review Technique 138

Bibliography 141

Index. 143

Improving
Individual
Performance

1

Introduction

Why Working with Individuals?

Groups are in vogue in training. Everywhere we look we see groups, group activities, group training techniques, group interaction, etc. When we enter a training classroom, we are likely to see one of three things happening: either a conventional lecture, a film, or a group exercise. When we view the current "training landscape," it is striking that not much has changed over the past twenty years. In some organizations, innovative training techniques are gaining a foothold. Computer-aided instruction, coaching, mentoring, and other approaches are making their appearance on the training scene. But, even today, probably 90 percent of all training largely involves a lecture, a film, or a group activity. The group appears to be today's "default value" in training. It seems as if there were an overriding principle in training: When in doubt, use a group activity.

Now, don't get me wrong. Groups are an excellent vehicle for learning. I have learned a lot from group activities, and, as a trainer, I enjoy using them. However, lectures, films, and groups are not the whole story. The literature on training is very sparse when it comes to dealing with techniques for training the *individual*. A lecture is an individual technique and so is a film, but this is a very limited range of options. The purpose of this book is to explore *a wide range of options available to trainers in working with individuals*. The purpose is not necessarily to encourage you to forsake group interaction for individual learning, nor to discourage you from using the lecture and film options (they have their place), but I have written this book to expand your options. I have written this book to share with you the many techniques that I (and others) have used successfully in working with individuals and in guiding them to higher levels of motivation, learning, and on-the-job application of what they have learned.

This book is about "freedom." Freedom is the availability of options and the courage to use them. A person who lives in a democratic society has a great deal of freedom, but this freedom is of no value unless it is used. We can so easily put ourselves in our own prisons by not knowing of, or using, our freedom. Unfortunately, many trainers do just this. They are unaware of the full range of training options available to them, and, even when they are aware, they often fail to take advantage of these options. So, this book is intended as a resource that you can use to expand your options. Don't just read it, *use it* together with the other books in this series, and you will have a freedom that you never before imagined possible.

What Does It Mean to Work with Individuals?

Classrooms are full of individuals. Groups are a collection of individuals. Ultimately, all learning is individual. It is impossible to talk about "group learning"; it just doesn't make sense! *A group cannot learn, only individuals can.* Learning takes place inside an individual's brain. Certainly groups can be a valuable tool to facilitate individual learning, but we must never lose sight of the fact that our focus must be on the *individual learner* and his or her performance. Unfortunately, I think that many trainers have lost sight of this fact.

"Working with individuals" means to understand the individual nature of learning. It means that we must not lose sight of the *personal responsibility* that must be taken by the individual learner and the responsibility that the trainer has for the learning of each individual trainee. Working with individuals involves a rediscovery of a type of learning with which we seem to have lost touch. Teachers used to recognize that learning was largely an individual process. Today we tend to make fun of the images of the "non-interactive" classroom. We think of a lack of group interaction as being indicative of backward and antiquated teaching. We have reacted against individual learning by going in pre-

Introduction

cisely the opposite direction, and, in the process, I believe we have over-reacted.

What Is an Individual Training Technique?

Most learning occurs in a classroom, in a group. Someday perhaps we will make enough progress in self-instruction and truly individualized learning that much learning will occur through one-on-one interaction between a learner and a range of learning resources (the trainer being only one resource). However, today, this is certainly not the case.

Many of the techniques suggested here may *appear* to be "group techniques," that is, they are generally used in a group setting. However, the setting is not important. Each technique in this book focuses on individual learning. In other words, the trainer and the individual trainee are interacting together, separate from other trainees. The fact that there are other trainees in the classroom is not a key consideration. None of the techniques reported in this book requires "group interaction." In some techniques, the possibility of expanding the technique to involve other trainees is mentioned. However, each and every technique can be run without any interactive involvement with others in the training group.

This greatly expands the trainer's options. Now, you not only have a wealth of techniques to use for group interactive learning, but you also have a rare collection of techniques for individual learning. This should greatly enhance your training effectiveness. That is the goal: *to increase your options and capacity to improve individual performance.*

The Advantages of Working with Individuals

Working with individuals is not only a method of expanding your training options. It also has some important advantages when compared with group interactive learning. Individual techniques are usually:
- Safer to use, since there are fewer "interactive variables" involved.
- Simpler to use, since there are few steps involved.
- Less disruptive to the flow of learning, since there is no need to break into groups.
- More flexible, since they can be implemented in any seting.

- More realistic, because so much of the work that people do is individual work, not group work.
- More powerful, because they focus on learning more directly, rather than on enjoyment or social experience.

The Importance of Individual Learning

Working with individuals means to recognize that learning is an individual process, even if it sometimes occurs in group settings. It means that we must not confuse "enjoyment" and "overt involvement" with "learning." Certainly enjoyment and involvement are important, but the bottom line is learning and performance. We must realize that individual learning can be just as enjoyable as group learning, and that "covert" involvement can be equally, or more, advantageous than "overt" involvement. Just because one doesn't see trainees "jumping around" the classroom or engaged in group discussion does not mean that the trainees are not involved. Covert, or internal, involvement is just as powerful a learning tool as overt, or external, involvement. It might not look as involving, because we expect to see groups interacting, but internal involvement is often more so. This is because the focus of the involvement is on enhancing learning, not on increasing enjoyment or the level of behavior. Computer-assisted, individualized learning holds a promise that is yet unrealized. Training may become increasingly "internalized." But, for the present, techniques, such as those presented in this book, are the best tools available for improving individual performance and accomplishment.

This book is a celebration of the lost art and science of individual learning. It derives from the recognition that it is what "happens inside" that is important, not what occurs outside. It is often the unobservable that is the key to learning and performance, not the amount of observed activity in the classroom. It is time we refocused our attention on where learning occurs and where performance begins: in the human brain.

The Essentials of Learning

Learning begins with some external stimulus. Through one or more of our senses, the human being *perceives* something. This

Introduction

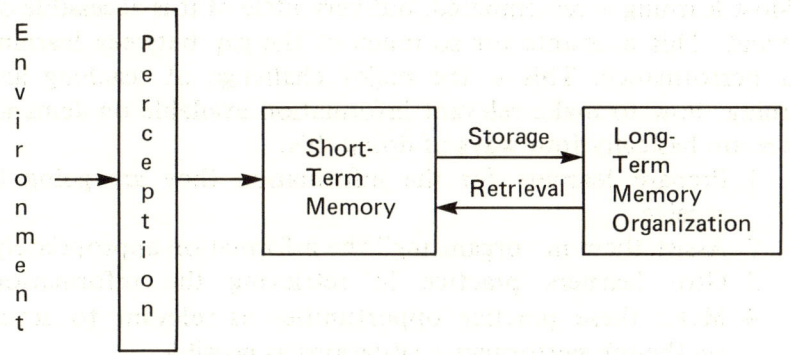

Figure 1. The Basic Processes of Learning.

perception is then transmitted to the brain. This *information* is usually held in the *short-term memory* for a brief period of seconds or minutes. At that point, it is either dropped from memory or goes into our *long-term memory*, where it is stored for future use. The three basic processes of learning are:
- Perception
- Short-term memory
- Long-term memory

All these are internal processes. See Figure 1.

When information reaches the long-term memory, it is stored in much the same way a computer stores information. Once information arrives in the long-term memory, it is almost always stored. The major problem of learning is not how to store information, but how to *retrieve* it. For instance, you might have a wonderful filing system in your business. Every paper that comes across your desk finds a place in your files somewhere. The important question is: Can you *find* each piece of paper when you need it? Retrieval, not storage, is the "bottom line" of filing! Our brains are wonderful storage mechanisms. They are full of information, but only some of that information is available to us when we need it. Often we remember things when we don't need them. This proves that the information is there but it does little to help us to be more effective in our lives.

Most learning is remembered, but very little of it is accessible on demand. This accounts for so much of the gap between learning and performance. This is the major challenge of teaching and learning: how to make relevant information available on demand. There are basically four ways of doing this:
1. Prepare learners for the information they are going to receive.
2. Assist them in "organizing" the information appropriately.
3. Give learners practice in retrieving the information.
4. Make these practice opportunities as relevant to actual on-the-job performance situations as possible.

Preparing Learners for Learning

One way to increase the likelihood that information will be accessible is to prepare a "proper" place for it in memory. This can be done through appropriate preparation of the learner for learning. Some of the methods that outstanding trainers use to do this are:
1. Informing the learner of the objectives of the lesson.
2. Stimulating interest in the information.
3. Creating interest in the lesson.
4. Making the information relevant to the learner's job.
5. Creating a positive attitude toward the learning experience.
6. Relaxing the learner.
7. Creating optimal conditions for learning.
8. Removing barriers to learning.

Encouraging Appropriate Organizing of Information

Once the ground-work has been laid for learning, it is important for learning to become personally relevant. Learning should be organized into "categories" that are meaningful to the learner, and consequently will have a better opportunity to be retrieved at some later date. This should involve a limiting of information, the creation of a personally relevant storage and retrieval system, and an effort to link new information with older information in a personally meaningful way.

Introduction

Some of the methods that outstanding trainers use to do this include:
1. Encouraging learners to focus on key information.
2. Demonstrating the relationship between new learning and previous learning.
3. Helping learners to see the relevance of learning to their personal lives.
4. Providing job-relevant examples.
5. Providing aids for memory.
6. Assisting learners to organize information.
7. Providing opportunities to review information.
8. Encouraging learners to challenge information.

Providing Opportunities for Practicing Information Retrieval

Once an appropriate storage and retrieval system has been established, it is still necessary to obtain practice in using it. Just as in using any system, practice will increase competence and confidence. No matter how good a library cataloging system might be, users still require practice in order to become effective and efficient users. No matter how well stored information may be in our memories, we still must have enough opportunity to practice retrieving it in appropriate situations, and to receive feedback about how well we did. With adequate practice and corresponding feedback, we are much more likely to be able to use appropriate information precisely when we need it.

The best trainers are able to provide this retrieval practice by:
1. Having learners repeat the information.
2. Developing realistic practice situations.
3. Providing opportunities for active learner response.
4. Reinforcing appropriate learner responses.
5. Encouraging learners to develop plans for using the information.
6. Providing successful experiences in using the information.
7. Providing links between using the information in the classroom and on the job.
8. Increasing learner commitment to using the information.
9. Preparing the performance environment for testing and refining newly acquired skills and information.

The Crucial Role of the Supervisor

There is no way to overestimate the role of the supervisor in ensuring the success of training. Continually, throughout this book, I reaffirm this importance. The supervisor is the major source of employee expectations, feedback, evaluation, rewards, punishments, and resources. The supervisor sets the tone for everything that is done (and not done) at work. Similarly, the supervisor is the crucial link in the performance system between the job and training. If a supervisor considers training to be important, so will the trainee. If the supervisor thinks that training is a waste of time, most probably so will the trainee. The attitudes of the supervisor can be the most important resource of the trainer, without which on-the-job results are a mere pipe-dream.

As training professionals, we cannot afford to overlook the importance of this usually unsung hero or villain of the entire training enterprise. I would go so far as to say that the supervisor is more critical to on-the-job results from training then even the trainer. In addition, I believe that the tone that is set before and after training by the supervisor is the key factor which determines the probability of success or failure.

You will find that many of the techniques presented in this book involve the trainee's supervisor. The attempt is to increase the likelihood that the supervisor will understand the importance of training, view it as job-relevant, and become a "part owner" in the performance improvement process. Supervisor-trainee meetings before training are important to help clarify expectations, and meetings after training are essential to increase transfer. These meetings need to be more than a charade. They need to be substantive.

Most training professionals who have dealt closely with large numbers of supervisors are aware that they tend to be conservative in their orientation, and their evaluation of work tends to focus on short-term productivity. This is only natural, since their own rewards depend upon it. One of the most important tasks for the trainer is to make training's immediate job-relevance clear to supervisors so that they can see the value for both trainees and themselves.

Introduction *11*

Organization of This Book

Given the foregoing discussion, the way in which this book is organized should not be surprising. The main body of the book is divided into four chapters. The first chapter includes techniques about how to prepare trainees for learning. The second includes techniques that encourage trainees to create the proper organizational system for learning. The third is concerned with techniques to facilitate appropriate practice and feedback. The fourth chapter provides techniques for evaluation.

Although I have not discussed evaluation as a major component of learning, it is crucial to effective training. We often take it for granted that our teaching will result in learning, and that all learning will result in appropriate performance. However, since all learning is internal, we will never be able to assess our success without effective evaluation. Evaluation makes the "internal" external. Evaluation enables trainers, managers, and learners to "see" learning, indirectly if not directly. As such, evaluation (although frequently overlooked) is just as critical an element of learning as the preparing, organizing, and practice.

Therefore, you can see that it is no coincidence that this book is divided into these four chapters:
1. Preparing for learning.
2. Organizing information.
3. Practice for retrieval.
4. Evaluation of learning.

Each of the four parts of the book contains a large number of training techniques. The presentation of each technique is divided into four sections. The first section is a, usually brief, statement of the *purpose* of the technique. The second section is a *description* of the technique, usually providing step-by-step instructions and some hints on how to use the technique more effectively. The third section discusses the *strengths and weaknesses* of using the technique. The fourth section provides some insight into the application of the technique: usually an *example* of how the technique was used by myself or another trainer to improve learning and performance.

How and Why the Techniques Were Selected

In selecting individual techniques for this book, my major motivation was to provide trainers with a *wealth of options*. That was the first and foremost goal. However, in order to make the book more valuable, it was necessary to select technique that had some previous "track record." In order to do this, I selected both from my own fifteen years of training and consulting experience, as well as from my network of contacts throughout the training profession. This was not an easy task. As I lamented above, the most popular training techniques involve group interaction. Discovering "individual techniques" involved some considerable digging. I have always valued the emphasis on the individual, and have been somewhat cautious of too much group involvement. That is one of the reasons why many of the techniques were personally developed and tested to respond to my own training situations and needs.

None of these techniques come from other books, although it is possible that others have co-invented them. Some of the ideas for these techniques come from the prolific literature on human learning and performance. Some of the techniques selected are more "established" and rather widely known and used; others are more experimental. The techniques were not selected because they are part of the "tool kit" of the average trainer. They were selected because of their demonstrated value to effective trainers who work in organizations like your own. They have all been shown to be useful methods of "improving individual performance" in actual training settings. They were selected because they are easy to use. They were selected because they involve a minimum of class disruption. They were selected because they can serve as the basis for individual trainer creativity.

My Responsibility and Your Responsibility

My responsibility in writing this book has been to select a wide range of techniques to assist trainers in working more effectively with individual trainees. It has also been my responsibility to explain these techniques as clearly as possible. I do not see it as my responsibility to "spoon feed" professional trainers. Therefore, I have often avoided the kind of detailed explanations that many trainers have come to expect in books such as this one. I have done this purposely.

I have taken this approach because I wanted to include as many techniques as possible, because I believe that this is the major rea-

Introduction

son for buying or reading a book of "techniques." I have taken this approach also because I believe that it is the responsibility of the individual trainer to make each technique "their own," your own. This is best done by encouraging you to adapt each technique to your own training goals and training setting. I have tried to be explicit enough without needlessly limiting individual creativity.

Every technique in this book can be used creatively to increase learning and improve performance. Every technique in this book can be applied to virtually any type of training or training objectives. Every technique in this book can be adapted to virtually any training setting. It has been my responsibility to stimulate you to do so. It is now your responsibility to make it happen!

Bibliography

At the end of the book you will find a bibliography of references. I hope that these references will enable you to further enhance your knowledge and skills in "working with individuals." A few of the authors and references have been mentioned in the text, but most references are of a general nature. Since this book is an "experiential" one, it has not been written on the basis of library research. It is based on *the actual experience of trainers and performance analysts*. The bibliography is not for the purpose of documenting the source of the techniques, but is intended to assist you in exploring further in the field of individual learning and performance.

Final Admonitions

So, there you have my introductory explanations, and "rationalizations"! I know that you will find this book to be a stimulating and useful reference. It is not a novel, and I would not recommend that you read it in one sitting. This book is a *resource*, and, as such, I hope you will constantly use it, refer to it, and share it with others.

This book is not intended to be a fool-proof recipe. Although most techniques are described in a step-by-step format, each technique should be personally adapted to the style and preferences of the individual trainer who uses it. Be active and creative in reading and using this book. Involve yourself in "rewriting" it to fit your own requirements and goals.

2

Preparing for Learning

In this chapter, you will find techniques to assist you in preparing trainees for getting the most out of learning. You will find techniques for:
1. Clarifying trainee expectations.
2. Involving supervisors in preparation for learning.
3. Emphasizing learning objectives.
4. Analyzing learner characteristics.
5. Relaxing trainees in preparation for learning.
6. Overcoming resistance to learning.
7. Creating a positive mental attitude toward learning.
8. Encouraging trainees to think about on-the-job application of what they are preparing to learn.

You can use one or many of these techniques to create "internal" (inside the learner) conditions and "external" (within the classroom) conditions that are most conducive to individual learning and performance.

PRE-COURSE TRAINEE-SUPERVISOR DISCUSSIONS TECHNIQUE

Purpose

This activity is intended to assist in clarifying trainee expectations before training. All too often, trainees are "dumped" into training programs without knowing why they are being sent and what they are supposed to do with their newly learned knowledge and skills when they return to the job. This type of activity contributes significantly to clearer trainee expectations, while simul-

Preparing for Learning 15

taneously increasing supervisor commitment to making the training process successful.

Description

A Pre-Course Trainee-Supervisor Discussion can be run in a great many ways. The following is simply a suggested method:
1. The trainer should encourage each trainee's supervisor to meet with the trainee prior to the beginning of the training program. This should occur approximately one to two weeks prior to the course. I recommend that this be cleared with the unit manager first, and that his or her support be obtained before announcing such a meeting.
2. The supervisor arranges an appointment with the trainee. This is not an activity to be done "on the run."
3. The discussion should cover the following issues:
   a. The relevance of course objectives to the trainee's job.
   b. The reasons why the trainee was selected for the course.
   c. What the trainee is expected to learn in the course.
   d. What the trainee is expected to do, as a result of attending the course, when he or she returns to the job.
4. It is recommended that both the supervisor and the trainee maintain a written record of this discussion, since it really constitutes a pre-course action plan.
5. The discussion should end in a positive and encouraging manner, providing the trainee with motivation to get the most out of the training experience and to anticipate returning to the job with the supervisor's full support for applying new knowledge and skills learned to the job.
6. There may be an advantage to "formalizing" this technique, and making it unit or company policy. There are strong arguments for selling unit managers on the idea and encouraging them to "institutionalize" it. Supervisors may view a voluntary meeting as unnecessary.

Strengths and Weaknesses

This is an extremely effective way to increase trainee and supervisor motivation to make the training process a more "results-oriented" one. Unfortunately, it is often difficult to gain supervisor enthusiasm for such an activity, and to encourage supervisors to take it seriously. If you can manage to obtain supervisor commitment (either voluntarily or through a policy directive), such a pre-course discussion can have extremely beneficial results.

Example

Pre-course discussions are now being widely used in a large paper products manufacturing organization to increase the results from training programs. Previously, this company experienced little pre-course communication between trainees and their supervisors. When trainees returned to the job with new knowledge and skills, they encountered little support from their supervisors or co-workers. As a consequence, excellently designed training programs often resulted in very little on-the-job performance improvement. A performance analysis showed that "supervisor sabotage" was one of the major problems. Common supervisor sabotage strategies included anything from ignoring that the training even took place to increasing the trainee's workload immediately on returning to the job. Pre-course discussions were adopted on a trial basis by one unit, after receiving the strong personal support of an influential manager. Gradually other units followed suit. The results have been very promising, with involved supervisors reporting considerably more favorable attitudes toward training and greater productivity on the job.

PRE-COURSE TRAINEE-TRAINER CONTACTS TECHNIQUE

Purpose

The purpose of Pre-Course Trainee-Trainer Contacts is to sensitize trainees to an upcoming training program and to clarify trainee expectations about its purpose and content. When trainees arrive at a training course, they are often ignorant of why they have been chosen, what the "real" purposes of the training program are, and what they are supposed to do with their new knowledge when they return to the job. It is extremely rare that trainees fully understand why they were chosen for this "honor." It is best to clarify these expectations and reduce anxiety prior to the program itself. This helps trainees release maximum positive energy *from the very start of the program*. It will also enable trainers to identify possible problems relating to on-the-job application of learning prior to the program, and to remedy these problems before it is too late.

Description
1. Announce that there will be a pre-course meeting for all trainees. Contact trainees' supervisors to clear their attendance. Experience has shown that scheduling these contacts approximately two weeks before the program provides excellent results.
2. At the meeting, explain to trainees the objectives of the course and elicit their feedback.
3. Provide trainees with an opportunity to share their background, their expectations, and their concerns about the training. Assure them that their comments will be strictly confidential.
4. Make it clear that the purpose of training is to improve on-the-job performance. The trainer should inquire about whether the trainee has any concerns about support back on the job.
5. If any serious concerns are raised, it may prove advantageous to contact relevant managers and supervisors to discuss these concerns, while not violating your pledge of confidentiality.
6. Create excitement and anticipation about the course. Provide trainees with background reading, if appropriate.

Strengths and Weaknesses
Pre-Course Trainer-Trainee Contacts can be very helpful for clarifying trainee expectations and reducing anxieties that could contribute to sabotaging the training program. It is always best to deal with these potential obstacles before they become real obstacles. It is also hazardous to enter into a training program without first having contact with the trainees. In addition, trainees generally react very positively to such a pre-course meeting. This preliminary contact enables the trainer to better prepare for the course, with far more knowledge of the target audience.

While there are many positives, there are also some potential concerns. For instance, such pre-course contacts may be difficult to implement if there is substantial geographical distance between trainees and the training site. In addition, considerable care needs to be taken with how such meetings are planned and managed, as the political ramifications can be significant. Implementing such meetings might require a change of policy.

Example

One Fortune 500 consumer products company has adopted Pre-Course Trainer-Trainee Contacts as a way of preparing the groundwork for more successful training. Previously, this organization found that trainees tended to come to training courses with widely diverse expectations. This situation required a considerable amount of "fixing" at the beginning of each course. Even after expectations were re-aligned, there were always some trainees who participated half-heartedly, expressing disappointment over the way the session began. By using pre-course meetings, this company was able to significantly increase the productivity of training and reduce much of the pre-course anxieties inherent in training situations when trainees arrive "cold."

Trainers reported two major benefits from using this technique: (1) trainees come to class much better prepared for actively participating in course activities, and (2) they arrive with a better set of attitudes toward the training topics. Managers report that trainers are less likely to be perceived as passive. When the training unit takes charge and implements a structure which demands active participation, trainees and their supervisors are more likely to respond appropriately.

TRAINING NEEDS QUESTIONNAIRE TECHNIQUE

Purpose

The purpose of a Training Needs Questionnaire is to learn more about the perceived needs for training, to obtain valuable information relevant to course design, and to get trainees to think about crucial training issues. Such a questionnaire can serve a great many useful purposes at once, while not requiring trainees to get together in person.

Description

A Training Needs Questionnaire is not a substitute for a full-blown needs analysis. It is a device that can be used to supplement needs analysis, while serving other purposes as well. It is suggested that such a questionnaire be developed and introduced according to the following general guidelines:
1. Clear the project with unit managers and trainees' supervisors.
2. Develop a standard questionnaire for all courses.
3. Ask only short-answer and multiple choice questions to facilitate trainee response, such as
   a. Which of the following best describes your reason for taking this course:
      ...... My supervisor told me to take it.
      ...... I need to improve my lathe operation skills.
      ...... I need some time away from the job.
      ...... I might learn something.
      ...... I have been asked to share new techniques with other employees in the unit.
   b. I am .... (describe your emotion) about attending this course.
   c. What do you perceive as the major problem you will have in implementing new lathe operation techniques when you return to the job?
      ...... I will receive little support from my supervisor.
      ...... I will receive little support from my co-workers.
      ...... Production schedules will not allow me time to apply what I learn.
      ...... Other: .... (please specify)
4. Ensure confidentiality, possibly by requesting the questionnaire be returned anonymously.

You might not receive 100 percent return, but the information you do get back will probably be very useful in preparing your approach to the training program and post-course follow-up. At the very least, you will become more aware of your constraints.

Strengths and Weaknesses

This technique can be very useful in acquiring information for pre-course planning. It is also most appropriate in settings where pre-course meetings are not feasible. However, there is the problem of the low rate of questionnaire returns and possible dubious accuracy of information. Such a questionnaire could be perceived as a threat by both trainees and supervisors. Its success is probably dependent upon the existing organizational climate and the trainer's reputation.

Example
Pre-course questionnaires have been successfully used in a large high-technology corporation, in which manufacturing facilities are de-centralized, but training is still centralized. Such questionnaires enable trainers to plan more thoroughly for each course prior to meeting with trainees. It is a standard procedure to distribute pre-course questionnaires for the first few times a new course is run and periodically thereafter to verify findings and query new/different trainee populations. Many potential problems have been anticipated and prevented by the use of this technique. For instance, in several cases, training programs had been used as a form of employee punishment by supervisors. The pre-course questionnaire identified this problem, and it was defused in time before the credibility of the training unit was seriously jeopardized. In another case, a training program was totally revamped prior to its scheduled debut, due to valuable pre-course feedback from a Training Needs Questionnaire. Much of this success was due to a supportive and responsive management team which was willing to listen to employee feedback.

PRELIMINARY EXERCISES TECHNIQUE

Purpose
Preliminary Exercises provide a potentially useful method for "sensitizing" trainees to the course subject matter before they attend the course itself. It is also a good way of finding out how much trainees know about the course content prior to the course. Again, it is important to obtain the blessings of the relevant managers and supervisors, but this should not be difficult to achieve.

Preparing for Learning 21

The idea is to get trainees thinking about the course while they are still on the job. This will provide a "bridge" between the job and the course.

Description
1. Develop a relevant exercise relating to the content of the course. This exercise should be brief, so that it is not perceived as being "in competition with" the course itself. Examples: A personnel problem that needs to be solved; a mechanical fault that needs repair (how would they do it?).
2. Obtain management/supervisor approval. Ask for the supervisor to discuss this assignment with trainees.
3. Distribute the exercise to trainees, either directly or through the trainee's supervisor. Indicate the reasons for the exercise and its importance to course preparation. Make sure that instructions are very clear. Give very clear guidelines for return of the exercise and deadline date.
4. Use the results of the exercise to help prepare for the course.
5. Thank trainees and supervisors for their cooperation.

Strengths and Weaknesses
Preliminary Exercises are extremely useful for preparing trainees for the training program and for obtaining additional information concerning their existing level of knowledge. However, as in other such pre-course techniques, there is a certain amount of inertia and threat that must be overcome. Trainees and supervisors must be convinced of the value of the exercise and its lack of potential threat. In addition, trainees must be given the time by their supervisors to complete the exercise. This is a key point which deserves emphasizing. Without the full support of supervisors (not just lipservice support), any technique that requires the trainee's time and effort on the job may be futile. With full supervisor support, Preliminary Exercises can greatly enhance preparation for training; without such support, they can be frustrating and counter-productive.

Example
Preliminary Exercises has been used most successfully in organizations which have customer service training needs. Customer

service problems seem to be most appropriate for the design of paper-and-pencil exercises since employees need to "work through" possible solutions. One company has developed a "data bank" of actual customer service problem situations that are used both for pre-course exercises and exercises during the course itself. When used before the course, these exercises have assisted the training staff in better targeting the course to the level of the trainees. Trainees have also indicated that completing these exercises has helped them begin thinking about the course content prior to the first class session. Trainees report that Preliminary Exercises give them a "greater sense of confidence" and "clearer expectations about the course" prior to the first class session. Supervisors are supportive of the approach now that they have seen the results. They report that the relatively short amount of time that it takes to complete the exercises has resulted in greater learning from the program without any increase in course length.

PRE-COURSE CONTRACT TECHNIQUE

Purpose
The purpose of a Pre-Course Contract is to create an agreement between trainees and their supervisors prior to the course. If effectively implemented, this will serve both to motivate trainees to take the training course more seriously and encourage supervisors to take a greater interest in the training of their subordinates.

Description
1. Develop a standard contract form. This can be easily modified to meet the needs of each type of course and the preferences of each supervisor. Such a form can be very simple and might include items such as the following:
   a. To prepare for the .... course, I will ....
   b. During the course I will make notes on how the course content applies to the job and share these notes with my supervisor.

Preparing for Learning 23

    c. Within one week of the end of the course I will make an appointment with my supervisor to discuss the course content and application to the job.
    d. I agree to share my observations about the course with other employees during the staff meeting on .... (date).
2. Discuss the contract with each supervisor involved. This can be done through a series of group seminars with supervisors throughout the organization.
3. Ask supervisors to complete the form with trainees at least two weeks prior to the course and commit themselves to reviewing it with trainees immediately after the course.
4. You may or may not ask supervisors to allow you to see the contract. This will depend on your relationship with the supervisors.
5. It is possible that the use of this technique might have to be cleared with managers and union officials.
6. A Pre-Course Contract does not have to be formally drafted, but can simply be an informal "understanding" between the trainee and the supervisor.

Strengths and Weaknesses

A Pre-Course Contract can be a useful device for focusing the trainee's attention on the importance of gaining the maximum benefit from the training course. It also makes explicit the supervisor's commitment to training and to application of new learning back on the job. It is the mutual acknowledgment of the importance of training and post-training follow-up that is important, not the technique itself.

It is important that such a "contract" not be perceived as punitive in any way. Perhaps "agreement" is a better term. The sensitivity with which the contract is presented to the trainee is critical to its success. Generally, such a technique will only work in an organization that already has a reasonably favorable climate, or in organizations in which structure is the hallmark of all agreements. It is easy for such contracts to be perceived as potentially threatening, and this appearance of threat must be reduced before the technique is implemented.

Example

An outstanding trainer in a medium-sized telecommunications firm has pioneered the use of this technique. She has designed a "contract" form that is acceptable to both trainees and supervisors in the company, and it is being widely used. See Figure 2. This has not only provided a structure for post-course follow-up, but it has also provided more focused trainee participation in the course itself. In several cases, trainees agreed to share the course content with other employees in their units. It is amazing how the "threat" of having to share the content with other employees has improved the quality of note-taking and questioning during the course.

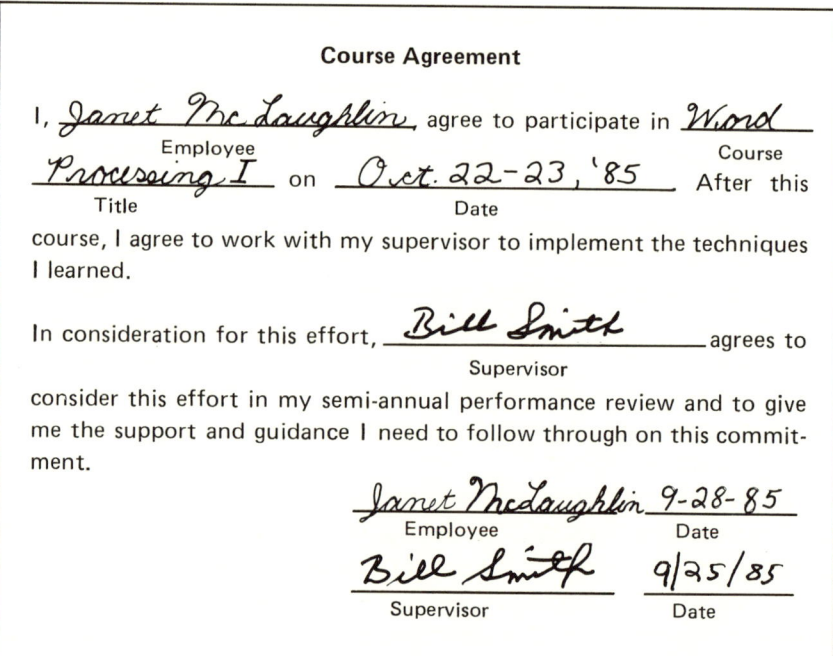

Figure 2. Sample Course Agreement

Preparing for Learning

SUPERVISOR BRIEFINGS TECHNIQUE

Purpose

It is impossible to over-emphasize the importance of the supervisor in performance improvement. The supervisor (or manager) is the key to training effectiveness. Supervisor Briefings are a way to increase likelihood that supervisors will work for training effectiveness, not against it. Supervisor Briefings underscore the critical importance of their role in the human performance system.

Description

Supervisory Briefings can be given for a single course or for a series of courses. The idea is to acquaint supervisors with the content of the course(s) their subordinates will be attending, to emphasize the critical role of supervisors before and after the course, and just to generally gain supervisory support for the training function. These briefings can be specific to a single course or can be more general in nature, depending on your own time constraints and needs. I tend to prefer supervisor briefings which are specific to each course. This way the content and requirements of the course can be made very clear in no uncertain terms.

Although there is not a strict format or procedure for such meetings, I tend to run them as follows:
1. Clear the idea with unit managers.
2. Send a cordial invitation to supervisors.
3. Follow-up with a telephone call.
4. At the meeting, cover the following content:
   a. The objectives of the course.
   b. Why the course was developed; why it is important.
   c. The importance of trainee preparation and follow-up.
   d. What happens when training is not followed-up on the job.
   e. The supervisor's critical role in training.
5. It is important to leave adequate time at the meeting for feedback from the supervisors.
6. Always be positive in your comments; never appear to be criticizing previous lack of supervisor support.

7. Be profuse in your thanks for their attendance, and show that you anticipate their support.
8. If your budget permits, I suggest that you incorporate such briefings with a meal function, or at least some refreshments.
9. A variation on this technique is Management Briefings, which is simply the same type of pre-course meeting aimed at managers. In such meetings, the emphasis tends to be on gaining a more general level of management support.

Strengths and Weaknesses

Supervisor Briefings can be an extremely effective method of gaining supervisor support for pre-course trainee preparation and post-course follow-up. I have found that such meetings are generally very well-received. However, one must be careful not to appear as if supervisors are being manipulated. It is important to be honest and up-front about everything. You may also find that, depending upon the nature of your organization and its climate, supervisors may be more or less resistant to the approach. From my experience, if supervisors are treated as professional, management-level people, they will respond positively to this all-too-unusual initiative. This is also a great opportunity to solicit suggestions from supervisors and solidify their commitment to implementation and training follow-up.

Example

Many organizations are currently using Supervisor Briefings as part of their pre-training activities. These organizations have found that their success depends largely on the personal "finesse" of the trainers implementing it. The success of this technique is highly correlated with the "maturity level" of the organization. It is hard to expect mature responses from supervisors if they are not treated as mature individuals within the organization. One organization in particular has had difficulty in implementing this technique because of a "climate of confrontation" that exists within the company. But this should come as no surprise to anyone.

Another organization, with units producing competitive products for the same market, has formed teams of supervisors that meet regularly with an assigned trainer. In this case, supervisors

Preparing for Learning 27

take a major role in shaping training expectations and strategy for courses affecting their subordinates. The trainer functions as a team consultant, not dominating the meeting, but eager to make his or her courses optimally effective. In this company, competition is seen as vital to the health of all aspects of the organization, and training is seen as an essential liaison among all levels of management.

RELAXATION 1: DEEP BREATHING TECHNIQUE

Purpose

Once trainees enter the classroom, it is important to encourage them to leave the "cares of the job" and the "pressures of the outside world" behind them. Although some "linear thinkers" may be resistant to relaxation exercises, I have found relaxation techniques to be of tremendous value at the beginning of training sessions. The first relaxation technique we will consider is also the easiest: Deep Breathing. It is a quick and easy method of unwinding before each training session. Whether we like to admit it or not, "uptightness" is an epidemic disease in the organizational world and it is antithetical to successful training.

Description

1. Ask trainees to sit in a comfortable position. It helps if you have comfortable chairs for them to sit on!
2. Ask trainees to start breathing deeply; that is, taking air as deeply as they can into their lungs, and exhaling it as completely as they can. Warn them that this should be a comfortable process and should not cause any strain on their part.
3. Now ask trainees to close their eyes and get as comfortable as possible, while continuing to breathe deeply, but naturally.
4. After a few trials, ask trainees to start inhaling and exhaling according to the following rhythm:

   "Inhale   1, 2
   Exhale   3, 4, 5, 6
   Inhale   1, 2
   Exhale   3, 4, 5, 6"

You should slowly read out the cadence in a calm relaxing man-manner.
5. Continue this process for about 3-5 minutes.
6. You can use soothing background music to further enhance relaxation.

Strengths and Weaknesses

If this technique is introduced with sensitivity and a sense of humor, it should result in only positive effects. The only problems might occur in organizations that are completely unaccustomed to anything out of the ordinary. Some might view this technique as weird "meditation" or too "touchy feely," but this will be the exception, not the rule. Explain the importance of relaxation to learning. Make relaxation part of your usual training procedure.

Example

A great many organizations, both government and private sector, are using techniques such as Deep Breathing as part of their preparation for training. Once trainees become acquainted with how fast and easy it is to relax, they respond very positively. One large computer company in particular has reported exceptionally positive results from the use of Deep Breathing at the beginning of each class session. This is a very traditional organization that has learned that sometimes it pays to be non-traditional! In another organization, Deep Breathing has proven so effective in training that it has been institutionalized in the workplace. Now it is being used as part of the normal work regimen of more than 300 employees who spend most of their time working at CRT's.

RELAXATION 2: PROGRESSIVE RELAXATION TECHNIQUE

Purpose

Progressive Relaxation is another very effective technique for helping trainees release themselves from the tensions of the outside world. The purpose is not to cause drowsiness, but to allow trainees to become maximally receptive to the content of the training course.

Description

1. Ask trainees to assume a comfortable position and close their eyes.
2. Advise trainees that this technique will involve them in tensing various parts of their body and then releasing the tension. Explain that they are already tense. This additional tension will enable them to focus on that tension and then release it more completely.
3. Start at the one extremity of the body and work to the other extremity. For instance, you might start by asking trainees to tense their forehead (as tense as they can make it), and then to release the tension. Then you gradually work downwards to their shoulders, their arms, their torso, their legs, and finally to their feet.
4. Continue this process until each major part of the body has been progressively tensed and relaxed.
5. Ask trainees to experience this relaxation for a few minutes before you tell them to open their eyes and begin the first training activity.
6. Again, an instrumental musical background can be helpful.

Strengths and Weaknesses

The same generalizations apply for this technique as for the previous one. Both techniques are extremely effective for relaxation. The only hazard might be a psychological resistance on the part of a few trainees to techniques such as these. It is up to the trainer to introduce the technique with sensitivity and even humor (humor is often a very effective antidote to resistance).

Example

I use Progressive Relaxation often in many seminars and courses I run. I have found both this and Deep Breathing to be extremely useful in reducing stress that might otherwise impede training effectiveness. Each technique takes only five minutes or so and the payoffs can be truly remarkable. A colleague has reported the successful use of Progressive Relaxation in training employees in jobs that require a high level of precision. In his organization, many assembly line workers need to make extremely precise manipulations throughout a prolonged working period. During training, Progressive Relaxation proved essential in providing quick relief from the high tension build-up. Introduced as part of the learning process, trainees are encouraged to continue using this relaxation technique once they complete training and return to use their new skills on the job.

ACKNOWLEDGING FEELINGS TECHNIQUE

Purpose
The purpose of this technique is to bring trainees' feelings out into the open at the beginning of a training course. This will release some of the anxieties, hostilities, and resentments that might otherwise serve to compromise the effectiveness of the program at a later time. It also presents an opportunity for the trainer to uncover, publicize and gain momentum from positive feelings that participants bring with them to a training session.

Description
1. Ask trainees to take out a blank piece of paper and write down five words that describe how they are feeling. You might want to show them what you mean by writing a few descriptive "feeling" words on an overhead transparency, such as "expectant," "anxious," "tired," "excited," etc.
2. Ask trainees to read out some of the words that they have written down, while you record them on overhead transparency sheets.
3. Discuss these words and how they relate to "normal" "feelings" which commonly emerge at the beginning of any training program. Acknowledge and reinforce feelings of excitement and anticipation. Don't dwell on negative feelings. Simply acknowledge their legitimacy, and move on.
4. Ask the trainees to acknowledge their feelings, accept them, but not let them impede their enjoyment of, or learning from, the training program.

Strengths and Weaknesses
This technique is very effective for "clearing the air" at the beginning of a training program. There are often feelings on the

Preparing for Learning

part of trainees that can adversely affect the training process unless they are dealt with early on. Of course there is always the danger that bringing up these feelings can cause an unintended explosion of negativity. This is rare, but, whenever one is dealing with hidden feelings, there are always some inherent dangers.

Example

The most effective trainers always attempt to deal with the emotional issues relating to training early in a training program. There are many examples of what happens when this has not been done, and the hostilities of individuals have boiled over and affected the entire group. A colleague of mine has reported several instances of individuals who were upset about having been "singled out" to attend unpopular courses, and spent much of the time venting their personal hostilities, seriously affecting the whole program. When Acknowledging Feelings was incorporated in the programs, and potentially hostile feelings are openly and honestly dealt with, these disruptions rarely occurred. My colleague also points out that trainees with "great expectations" may have been disappointed if he had not understood their feelings at the start of training. Often, it is the little things that make a difference and minor adaptations in plans can make a world of difference in satisfying excited or "event-conscious" trainees.

CREATIVE NAME TAGS TECHNIQUE

Purpose

This technique is intended to be a "warm up" activity at the beginning of a training course. Creative Name Tags provides trainees with an opportunity to assert their individuality, to be a little bit creative, and to relax in preparation for the start of the formal program.

Description

1. Ask trainees to take name tags (which are available in various colors).
2. Ask trainees to take colored markers and design their own creative name tags.

3. One variation on this technique is to offer a prize for the most inventive name tags.

Strengths and Weaknesses

This technique is a very good one for "starting things rolling" in the course. It helps relax trainees and warm them up for the training program proper. It is possible that some trainees might view this activity as "Mickey Mouse," and be turned off by it. However, this has not been my experience.

Example

I have seen Creative Name Tags work extremely well in warming up hourly factory workers who generally feel uncomfortable in a formal training setting. On a number of occasions, this activity has been successful with mill foremen. It has served to "break the ice," bring out the best in these employees, and help them begin to grasp their own creative (and expressive) potential. These "great big brutes" turned into a bunch of creative "pussy cats," each one trying to outdo the other in an opening "name tag competition."

ENVIRONMENTAL ENRICHMENT TECHNIQUE

Purpose

The purpose of Environmental Enrichment is to bring out the creative potential of trainees and to provide a stimulating setting for the training program. Considerable research has shown that the training environment can have a very powerful effect on learning and performance. Too often, classrooms are drab, colorless, and depressing places that do little to stimulate excitement. They all tend to look alike. Environmental Enrichment attempts to change that, and add a little spice to trainees' lives.

Description

This technique involves the creation of a stimulating, exciting, and unusual environment within the training classroom. This can be done in any number of ways, including:

1. Painting the room in colorful patterns.
2. Placing artistic prints around the room.
3. Using novel furniture and displaying art objects.
4. Playing relaxing, mood music during breaks in the program.

Strengths and Weaknesses

Why does training need to be drab and boring? Why do classrooms need to look like hospital wards? They don't! Environmental Enrichment is an idea whose time has come. I cannot think of a single reason for not doing it, other than the conservatism of stodgy managers.

Example

Unfortunately, there are few examples of Environmental Enrichment to draw upon at the present time. Most organizations either have not thought about it, or are too rigid to try it. Lozanov, in his work on "Suggestology," and Barzakov in his "Optimalearning," are two Bulgarian leaders in the area of environmental enrichment of learning settings. This technique has proved extremely successful in the experimental training work pioneered by these two men. I attended a fabulous training program run by Ivan Barzakov in which he modeled the use of Environmental Enrichment. The room was light and airy. There were beautiful art prints on the walls and on stands around the room. When we entered the room and during breaks, relaxing piano music would be playing. Barzakov turned what could have been a mundane training event into an experience to be remembered!

PERSONAL NEEDS ANALYSIS TECHNIQUE

Purpose

Although complete individualization of training is virtually impossible in traditional classroom settings, it is possible to make some strides toward greater personal relevance of training. Personal Needs Analysis is a step in this direction. The idea of this technique is to provide trainers with valuable data on trainees early in the course and to inform trainees that trainers are concerned about each trainee's personal needs. Too often training is perceived to be pre-packaged and inflexible. This technique, when appropriately used, will make training less so. This technique is particularly useful when it has not been possible to do a complete needs analysis prior to the course.

Description
1. Personal Needs Analysis can be accomplished by using a paper-and-pencil instrument or by group discussion. Because this book is about individual performance, I will suggest the paper-and-pencil method, although group discussion has the advantage of group synergy. See Figure 3.
2. Design a brief questionnaire instrument. I would suggest items such as the following:
    a. What are your primary learning objectives in this course?
    b. What are the two (or three) major problems you perceive on the job relating to .... (the course subject matter).
    c. What additional information do you want to learn about .... (course subject matter).
    d. Which of the course objectives do you feel are most relevant/irrelevant to your personal job performance needs?

    The answers to these questions can provide you with simple and valuable information on trainees to assist in structuring the course more precisely to their needs.
4. If the Personal Needs Analysis questionnaire is completed before the first class meeting, it is no problem to analyze the data (if indeed you get the returns). If the questionnaire is completed at the beginning of the first class session, I recommend that a colleague analyze the data while you are "warming up" the trainees. A simple questionnaire, such as this one, can be analyzed in about 15 minutes.
5. The results of the Personal Needs Analysis can be presented to the class for brief discussion, but this is not necessary. It is primarily an individual technique intended for the information of the trainer and to indicate your concern for individual trainee needs.

PERSONAL NEEDS ANALYSIS

Time Management _____ _Connie Rawls_ _____
Course   Employee

1. My primary learning objectives:

   To free two productive hours/week.
   To reduce procrastination.
   To complete sales survey by March 30.

2. My possible problem areas:

   Lack of boss' support.
   High work pressure this time of year.
   Lack of incentive.

3. Additional information I want to learn:

   How to work more closely with my secretary.
   Avoiding unnecessary interruptions

Figure 3. Example of Personal Needs Analysis.

Strengths and Weaknesses

The Personal Needs Analysis technique is particularly valuable when you have not had a chance to do a real needs analysis prior to the course and when you are not fully aware of the characteristics of the audience. When this is the case, a simple questionnaire approach can be extremely beneficial. The advantage of having the questionnaire completed in class is that you are certain to receive a 100 percent return, which is extremely unusual with questionaires. However, there is always a strong possibility that the results you receive will not be complete and fully accurate. Particularly during the early stages of the program, trainees may be less than fully candid, as they are intent on "psyching out" the situation. This is always a concern with this type of data collection. Whatever the results, you will find that the Personal Needs Analysis will yield useful data that will be far superior to no data at all.

Example

A number of organizations are using Personal Needs Analysis instruments to obtain information prior to the first session of training courses, when formal needs analyses are impractical. A training unit in a major manufacturing organization, with plants spread throughout the United States, has used this technique to "get more in touch with" their employees' training needs. Due to geographical constraints and other logistical considerations, it was difficult for this training unit to perform a full-scale needs analysis prior to a number of their courses. The Personal Needs Analysis, although a compromise solution, has enabled this unit to respond to employee needs with a minimal expenditure of time or effort. Consequently, the necessary information could be obtained, while adequate resources could be applied to course development.

COMPETENCY VISIONING TECHNIQUE

Purpose

Competency Visioning is a technique for motivating trainees to strive for optimal performance. It basically involves trainees creating a mental image of success, under the guidance of the trainer.

Preparing for Learning 37

Competency Visioning tends to form an expectancy of competent performance and starts the training program off on a very positive note.

Description
1. Ask trainees to sit in a comfortable position and to close their eyes. You might want to precede this activity with a relaxation exercise. Playing soft, relaxing background piano music might also enhance the effectiveness of this technique.
2. When the trainees are adequately relaxed, ask them to try to see themselves performing the task or skills described in the terminal performance objective. Describe competent performance to them in a relaxed voice, possibly in concert with background music. Describe competency in a very specific situation. However, do not become overburdened with detail. The trainer only needs to "set the stage." It is up to the individual trainee to "fill in" the picture.
3. After this has been done and you have allowed time for the trainees to appreciate the image, give them a little time to simply relax with their eyes closed. Then, ask them to gradually open their eyes. It is a good idea to dim the lights in the training room, so that opening their eyes will not shock the trainees ouf of this relaxing state.

Strengths and Weaknesses
Competency Visioning will make a set of impersonal, dry objectives come alive. Suddenly training objectives will have personal meaning to trainees as they begin to "see" them in their own mind's eye. On the other hand, trainees might view this activity as a bit contrived. It really depends on how sensitively the technique is introduced. When it is well implemented, Competency Visioning can have spectacular results.

Example
One computer company has used Competency Visioning successfully in training its sales and service representatives. The visions of competency have been developed through observing and interviewing "exemplary performers." The "visions" reflect the

customer service techniques that are taught in the training course. It has been demonstrated that the "gestalt" of sales and customer service activities requires a "visceral" ability to empathize with the customer problems and concerns. Competency Visioning helps increase this empathy in a classroom setting and during live customer interfaces. Trainees in this organization have reported on end-of course evaluation questionnaires that, as a result of this technique, course objectives have become clearer, motivation more focused, and competency significantly higher than before the technique was introduced.

SELF-AFFIRMATION TECHNIQUE

Purpose

Self-Affirmation is another technique that can significantly increase trainee motivation during the early stages of training. This technique should be a familiar one to those who are well-read in the literature on motivation. The technique basically involves the repetition of positive affirmations about oneself and the performance situation in which the person is about to engage. It creates positive expectancy and tends to overcome resistance to change.

Description
1. Ask trainees to assume a comfortable position. You may use a relaxation exercise prior to using the Self-Affirmation technique.
2. Ask trainees to write down some self-affirmations relating to the course. You might want to give them some examples on an overhead transparency, such as:
   - I want to learn ....
   - I know I will learn ....
   - I feel relaxed and wide awake.
   - I am confident in my skills.
   - Nothing can keep me from learning ....
   - I am going to enjoy and benefit from this training program.
3. Give trainees a few minutes to complete their list.
4. Ask trainees to read their list over to themselves several times.

5. Optionally, you may ask trainees to share their self-affirmations, as you record them on an overhead transparency sheet.
6. Sometimes a Self-Affirmation recording sheet has already been prepared for trainees (with course relevant examples), and is provided in the trainee's course hand-out materials.

Strengths and Weaknesses

Self-Affirmation is an extremely powerful technique for creating positive "success" feelings in trainees at the beginning of a training program. However, like all such motivational techniques, it can be taken negatively by people who are not "in tune" with this kind of technique. There are some who believe that these techniques are manipulative and "too psychological." There is no easy way to overcome this resistance, other than to acquaint trainees with such techniques and allow them to experience their effectiveness. However, one should bear in mind that, because this technique is an individual one, a negative overt "group reaction" can mask a positive covert, individual one.

Example

Self-Affirmations are most widely used in sales training, where both trainees and trainers are more familiar with such motivational methods. It would be unfortunate if we were to limit such a powerful technique to only those who are already familiar with its effectiveness. A number of sales trainers are successfully using Self-Affirmations in their training programs. Some use it throughout the course, not only at the beginning. They have found that the continued use of Self-Affirmations not only enhances learning, but is also effective as a powerful motivational technology that can be used in the trainee's daily work. In fact, a large copier manufacturer provides its sales representatives with audiotapes that stress positive self-affirmations.

OVERVIEWING TECHNIQUE

Purpose

It is positively mind-boggling how many times I have observed trainers who fail to provide an adequate overview of a training program at the beginning of the course. One of the most important preparatory activities must be to provide participants with a complete overview of course content and methods, not just with course objectives. Overviewing is a technique for doing precisely that.

Description

1. Give a clear list of course objectives. Try to limit this list to five or fewer. We often overwhelm trainees with objectives, as if we were trying to impress them by how much we can write about the course!
2. Show trainees how course activities are designed to help them achieve the objectives. I generally do this by way of a "course map" with each objective at the top of a tree-like diagram. See Figure 4.
3. Briefly explain each activity.
4. Briefly describe how the course was developed to optimize learning.
5. Allow trainees to ask questions and give them clear and concise answers.

Strengths and Weaknesses

Overviewing is a very important activity that is too often neglected in training designs. Just 10-15 minutes of Overviewing can avoid many problems later on. Trainees will come away with a much clearer understanding of the course and its design than they usually do. This will reduce anxiety and enhance motivation. I cannot think of a single weakness of this technique, if it is implemented appropriately. However, make sure that your objectives and "course maps" are simple, clear, and avoid any unnecessary jargon.

Example

Without exception, the best trainers I have observed are the ones that make their expectations clear *up-front*. First impressions

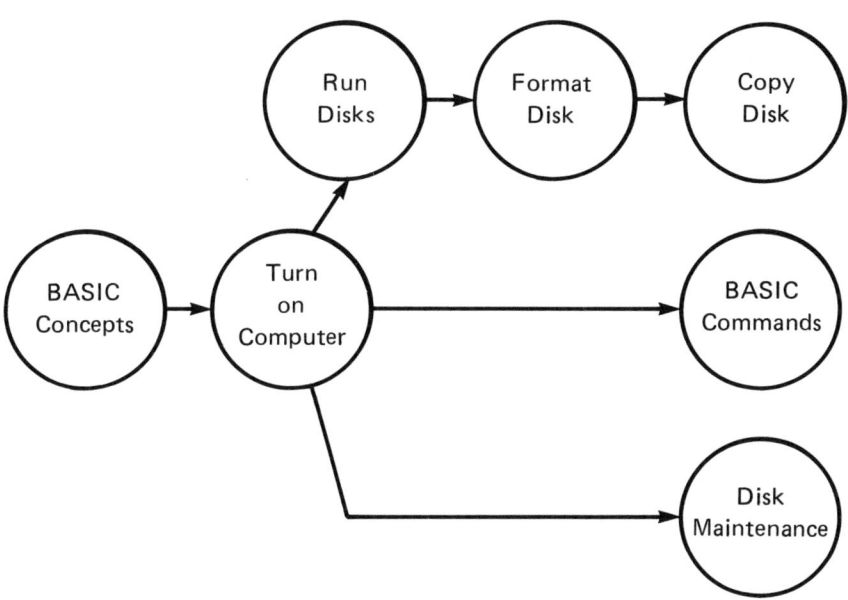

Figure 4. Example of a Course Map.

are critical, and the best trainers make the best first impressions. I have worked with many trainers who failed to adequately "overview" at the beginning of their courses. When they started overviewing, not only did their trainees express a greater understanding and confidence, but so did they!

This was never more true than in the case of a well-respected senior colleague who had formed the "bad habit" of skipping objective-setting in preference of less substantive activities. The audience enjoyed his personality but complained about lack of direction. When these complaints came to the attention of his manager, he was forced to reconsider his approach. Overviewing again became part of his standard, and successful, repertoire of training techniques. No more trainee complaints were heard about "lack of direction."

PRE-COURSE ACTION PLANNING TECHNIQUE

Purpose

Most of us are familiar with post-course action planning, but Pre-Course Action Planning is rarely used. The idea is to set the stage for more meaningful learning at the beginning of the course, rather than wait for it until the end. In this technique, trainees complete an "action planning form" at the beginning of the first class session to guide and motivate their learning throughout the course.

Description

1. Pass out a pre-designed Action Plan form. See Figure 5. I generally recommend that the forms have two columns: one for actions and one for schedule. However, for Pre-Course Action Planning, I generally only ask trainees to complete the "action" column. At this time, scheduling the actions is probably premature.
2. Ask trainees to determine what they intend to do after the course to implement the new knowledge and skills they intend to learn. Advise trainees to write these actions in the appropriate column on the Action Plan form. Emphasize the importance of listing specific actions no matter how insignificant they may seem.
3. You might ask trainees to share their proposed actions with the group, but this is not necessary.
4. Ask trainees to hold on to their Action Plans so that they can compare their Pre-Course and Post-Course Action Plans.

Strengths and Weaknesses

Pre-Course Action Planning can be very useful in helping trainees to start thinking early in the course about on-the-job application (undoubtedly the most important concept in training). It is never too early to get participants to focus on this subject. However, we should be aware that, at this point, trainees have very little information about post-course competency. Therefore, it is not always easy to complete a Pre-Course Action Plan. In my opinion, the difficulty in completing such a plan is not a serious draw-

ACTION PLAN

Action Steps	Schedule
DISCUSS COURSE WITH BOSS	MON. AUG 26
TRY NEW COMMUNICATION SKILLS IN MEETING	WED. SEPT. 4
USE POSITIVE DISCIPLINE	AT LEAST 2 × PER WEEK
GIVE BETTER FEEDBACK	AT LEAST ONCE A DAY

Figure 5. Sample Action Form.

back of the technique. The important thing is focusing attention on *action* as soon as possible in the course.

Example

In most training programs I lead, I try to incorporate some form of Pre-Course Action Planning. This is largely a consequence of my continual concern with on-the-job application, which I view as still the most neglected aspect of training. No training program can ever be really successful unless trainees are thoroughly committed to using their new skills on the job and are aware of how to go about doing so.

Of course, the impact of Pre-Course Action Planning is strengthened considerably when the organization commits itself to post-training performance support back on the job. A large security systems sales and service organization fed data on the relationship between training and "bottom line" performance measures to managers. Once this "link" became clear, action planning became an established, carefully conceived pre-course training activity. In this organization, training and performance are virtually synonymous.

PERSONAL PERFORMANCE ANALYSIS TECHNIQUE

Purpose

Personal Performance Analysis is a technique modeled on the "performance analysis" described by Gilbert (1978) in his book *Human Competence*. It is intended to get trainees to think systematically about the nature of their job at the beginning of a training course. This will help to clarify trainee expectations, provide trainers with a wealth of job-related information, and increase the likelihood that trainees will apply new learning to their jobs.

Description

1. Distribute "Personal Performance Analysis" forms. See Figure 6. These forms have four columns: Tasks, Accomplishments, Standards, and Performance Requirements.
2. Ask participants to first list as many of their job tasks as they can think of. These relate to the purposes of training and subsequent performance. Give them examples of these on an overhead transparency sheet, if necessary.
3. Ask participants to continue to complete the form column by column. You can continue to give relevant examples before trainees attempt to complete each column.
4. When the form is completed, you might want to spend a little time discussing the results, but this is not essential.
5. You might also want to include such job-related factors as personnel interrelationships, authority versus responsibility, and perceived obstacles in the work environment as part of the analysis. It is useful to expose these issues early in the training process, rather than them to sabotage training effectiveness later.

	Personal Performance Analysis		
Course:	CUSTOMER SERVICE REP.		
Tasks	Accomplishments	Standards	Performance Requirements
GREET CLIENT	CLIENT IS RELAXED AND OPEN	ASK AND ANSWER WITHOUT DELAY	FRIENDLINESS VERBAL AND NON-VERBAL COMMUNICATION SKILLS
COMPLETE COMPLAINT REPORTS	ACCURATELY COMPLETED REPORTS	NO ERRORS COMPLETED BY END OF DAY	KNOWLEDGE OF REPORT PROCEDURE AND COMPLAINTS
DEBRIEF CLIENT	NO RETURNING CLIENTS TO COMPLAINT DEPARTMENT	CLIENT CAN REPEAT BACK INFORMATION CORRECTLY	SKILL IN TACTFUL DE-BRIEFING, KNOWLEDGE OF PERTINENT INFO

Figure 6. Example of Personal Performance Analysis.

6. Do not worry about completeness. The object of the exercise is to start trainees thinking about the nature of their jobs, not to become performance analysts.

Strengths and Weaknesses

Personal Performance Analysis can be an effective technique for focusing trainee attention on the key dimensions of their jobs and work tasks. Most trainees will come away from this exercise with a much deeper understanding of the nature of their work and appropriate job expectations. However, this is a complex and difficult activity. If it is explained clearly with good examples, this should not pose a serious problem. Otherwise you might have to limit its application to "higher level" training programs. While some trainees might view Personal Performance Analysis as theoretical, it is up to the trainer to make it "nitty gritty" and job-relevant.

Example

Too many training programs are run without an adequate contextual understanding on the part of trainees. It is difficult for trainees to understand the relevance of training if they don't even understand the real nature of their jobs and performance expectations. A large food processing company has incorporated Personal Performance Analysis successfully in a wide range of training applications. They have found it most effective with clerical, administrative, and management-level employees who interface directly with line operations. In a trial application with hourly employees, it was predicted that difficulties would occur in their understanding of the performance analysis concepts. However, this problem did not come to pass. Trainers discovered, to their pleasant surprise, that even factory workers are capable of a much higher level of job knowledge and understanding of performance expectations than we usually give them credit for being able to attain.

PERSONAL OBJECTIVE REVIEW TECHNIQUE

Purpose

Course objectives are often presented to trainees in a perfunctory manner, without any apparent concern for understanding. Personal Objective Review is a technique for ensuring that partici-

Preparing for Learning 47

pants understand objectives and that objectives are personally meaningful to them.

Description
1. Distribute course objectives to trainees. Keep the number of objectives as low as possible. Leave adequate space between the objectives so that trainees have room to write.
2. Ask trainees to rewrite the objectives in their own words. This will force trainees to actively read the objectives, process them, and make them their own.
3. Optionally, you can ask trainees to rank the newly rewritten objectives in terms of personal relevance. This will motivate further active processing of the objectives and cause trainees to think deeper about personal applicability.
4. Again, at your discretion, you can open up the floor to discussion, or leave the exercise at this point if you prefer (or if time constraints dictate).

Strengths and Weaknesses
Personal Objective Review is a very useful technique for stimulating a more active review of objectives than usually occurs. I often wonder why trainers even give objectives, since they are almost always ignored. This creates a very bad impression for trainees. If this technique is adequately introduced and explained, I cannot think of a single weakness inherent in its use.

Example
One trainer with a Fortune 500 company had been frustrated by the apparent futility of providing objectives at the beginning of her courses. She had learned in graduate school that objectives were an essential element in instructional design. With limited success, she vainly sought to find a way to make course objectives more relevant to trainees. She now uses Personal Objective Review in every course she runs as a way to ensure that course objectives receive the emphasis they deserve. Trainees who had previously been "turned off" by training objectives (which may have been relevant to trainers but not to them), reported that they "finally" understood the purpose of the courses they took and what the

training department was trying to achieve. This trainer reported that a key factor in making objective relevant is to *insist* that trainees understand each objective despite apparent resistance. Almost always, trainees respond by taking the exercise seriously.

3

——— Organizing Information ———

In this part of the book, you will discover techniques for assisting trainees to organize information so that it will be more thoroughly retained and more easily retrieved when they need it. You will find techniques that will assist you in:
1. Presenting information so that it has a more personal impact on trainees.
2. Presenting information that is more interesting and more relevant.
3. More clearly showing the relationship among subject matter elements.
4. Emphasizing the most important information.
5. Guiding trainees to process information more actively and more personally.
6. Reinforcing and consolidating learning.

By using these techniques, you will be able to establish conditions which will optimize retention and increase the likelihood that trainees will be able to return to the job and apply the information and skills they learn at the proper time.

MULTI-METHOD PRESENTATION TECHNIQUE

Purpose
The purpose of Multi-Method Presentation is to provide trainees with learning experiences which will be received through several different senses (rather than just through one). These will tend to be more motivating, more completely processed by the brain, and therefore more thoroughly retained.

Description

Multi-Method Presentation is not really a technique so much as a class of presentation methods, and, as such, it is not conducive to step-by-step description. The guiding principle behind Multi-Method Presentation is that learning quality can be increased through the use of many different presentation methods used simultaneously or consecutively. Some of the methods that can be used to enhance learning and retention are:

1. Lecture
2. Discussion
3. Demonstration
4. Slides
5. Audiotapes
6. Videotapes
7. Overhead transparencies
8. Flip-charts
9. Role-plays
10. Self-instruction

Multi-Method Presentation encourages the trainer to use many teaching methods in the same learning activity. For instance, a trainer might introduce the subject by way of a brief lecture, then illustrate it with slides and audiotape, show the details on overhead transparencies, provide a self-instructional package on key concepts, then lead a discussion on the subject, and end with a review lecture. Every method of instruction has its unique value. When used appropriately and in concert, a number of different methods can have an extremely powerful impact, much more so than the use of one method alone.

Not only can Multi-Method Presentation provide different pieces of information in the most appropriate manner, but it can also present the same information in a way that will reinforce the content. Presenting the same concepts using more than one medium can provide valuable redundancy and highlight the most important material.

Strengths and Weaknesses

Unfortunately, most trainers tend to be extremely conservative and, in fact, routinely boring in their use of instructional methods.

There often seems to be a reluctance to try anything new. Multi-Method Presentation is an instructional strategy that encourages experimentation with a number of methods at once, within the same subject matter presentation. Each medium has its own unique strengths and limitations. Trainers can use different types of visuals to enhance learning, while still relying on verbal explanations to describe and highlight key points. Words, pictures, and other appropriately used media can be particularly valuable when used together to do what each does best.

Obviously, one of the major drawbacks to Multi-Method Presentation is the amount of planning and preparation that goes into it. This effort is most readily justifiable when the course is going to be repeated many times. It might not be justified for a one-time offering. Multi-Method Presentation is most useful when you want to make a strong impact on trainees. When used appropriately, it will do just that.

Example

Multi-Method Presentation has been used with extraordinary success in several new employee-orientation programs I have observed. In one such program in a Fortune 500 consumer products company, the trainer provided a slide-tape introduction to the company, followed by a lecture welcome, showed transparencies of organizational functions and structure, followed by videotape vignettes of key functional areas, and closed with a discussion. This was one of the most effective teaching sessions I have ever attended. Not only did it make a tremendous impression on new employees, but it continued to excite seasoned employees who were participating in the orientation program. The program acquired such a reputation for showcasing the organization's attributes that it is now used as part of "celebration sessions" to reinforce good feelings and promote excitement.

MOCK INTERVIEW TECHNIQUE

Purpose

The purpose of the Mock Interview is to provide a stimulating change of pace from the traditional lecture format of instruction. It is also an easy, but effective way to dramatize important subject matter and make it more memorable.

Description
1. Select the interviewer, who could either be a trainee or another trainer. Select a trainee to be the interviewee. Other trainees are given instructions on how to be effective observers.
2. Brief the interviewer, and give him or her a question script. Advise the interviewer that he or she can deviate from the script.
3. Set the stage for the interview.
4. Run the interview.

Strengths and Weaknesses

This technique is a method of adding "spice" to subject matter that might otherwise be presented exclusively by lecture. The Mock Interview will provide a change of pace. Virtually any subject matter that can be presented by lecture can also be presented using an interview format. The questions that are given, and your responses, can ensure that the content is fully covered. Allowing a little interviewer flexibility adds a bit of fun to the exercise.

The Mock Interview may remove some control from the presentation, which can cause some anxiety for the trainer who is unfamiliar with this technique. This technique also requires some contingency planning, just in case something goes haywire. However, with minimal planning, the Mock Interview can add a great deal to what might otherwise be a dry lesson.

Example

"This interview depicts a discussion between a maintenance engineer and his supervisor. An industrial accident has occurred, and the supervisor is exploring the reasons why it happened. I am the engineer. The interviewer is my supervisor." From that point, the

Mock Interview progressed, giving the trainer the opportunity to raise important points on how *not* to prevent an industrial accident. As the maintenance engineer, the trainer identified his "reasons" for the accident, offered explanations for his behavior and drew attention to his failure to utilize decision-making resources and recognize danger signals. This was followed up by a discussion with the class, highlighting the steps that should have been taken but were not.

In any "real-time" work environment, the risks and excitement are so much a part of the job that conventional lecture approaches to instruction usually fall short of trainee expectations and desired activity level. However, the Mock Interview technique is an easy way for the trainer to offer a more convincing and exciting classroom experience with clear on-the-job performance ramifications.

DRILL PRACTICE TECHNIQUE

Purpose
The purpose of Drill Practice is to increase the likelihood that key information or task steps will be retained after training. Drill practice can occur at regular intervals during the course, whenever there is something raised that must be remembered.

Description
1. When you reach a particularly critical point in the presentation, stop.
2. Ask trainees to practice that one point or step by repeating it over and over with you at least several times.
3. Continue this practice until you are confident that the trainees have mastered it.

Strengths and Weaknesses
Drill Practice is a simple method for increasing retention of important points and task steps. It can be used at any time to reinforce something that must be remembered. From the trainer's point of view, it requires a sensitivity to how much Drill Practice

is necessary before moving on to the next point. Using this technique may cause some discontinuity in the flow of the subject matter presentation, and some trainees might find this activity a bit boring. However, such complaints are generally overcome when trainees experience the enhanced learning that results. It is useful to incorporate opportunities for trainees to measure retention so the advantages of Drill Practice become readily apparent. Brief question/answer exchanges or "surprise" requests for on-the-spot responses (verbal, written or physical) can be very convincing.

Example

Drill Practice is most useful when there is a series of sub-skills to be learned. For example, a fellow trainer has used this technique very effectively in teaching word processing skills. When a new series of key-strokes are introduced, the trainees practice them repeatedly, while verbalizing their actions and the function, until they have memorized the sequence. "Control V, insert; control V, insert; control V, insert; control V, insert . . ." This process continues until the trainer is confident that each trainee understands what he or she is expected to do before inserting text. Trainees taking part in Drill Practice demonstrated a 25 percent increase in word processing speed, during the early stages of learning, in comparison with those who had not had the benefit of the Drill Practice activity.

HUMOR TECHNIQUE

Purpose

Humor can be extremely effective when used appropriately to enhance attention, learning, and retention. Humor involves a whole range of techniques, not just one.

Description

Many training sessions tend to be boring and lifeless. The most effective trainers I know have learned to use humor in their courses for optimizing learning. Some of the humorous techniques that might be used include:

1. Overhead transparency cartoons.
2. Humorous stories that illustrate teaching points.
3. Exaggeration.
4. A humorous film.
5. Coming to class in costume.
6. Humorous classroom decorations.
7. A surprise package filled with humorous, but job-relevant objects.

The list could go on virtually forever. The idea is simply to provide an experience that is light and *unexpected*. It is not hard to liven up a training session, because trainees expect the routine. When they get something out of the ordinary, they are quite pleased. And, despite the fact that the group often laughs together, the memories of humor and its effects represent a highly personal experience.

Strengths and Weaknesses

Humor is a very effective teaching tool that can alleviate boredom and make a mundane training session memorable. The only limitations of this "technique" is the trainer's imagination. However, care must be taken not to overdo humor in training programs, to ensure relevance, and to avoid too much disruption in the flow of learning.

Example

Some trainers are just "naturally" funny. I know a few of these, and envy their gift. Most trainers are like me, simply teachers, rather than comedians. So, it is useful to learn to use humor from time to time to liven up the session. I like to use humorous role plays and cartoons from time to time, and I find that a funny film adds a lot to a training session. These teaching aids tend to relieve tension and compensate for the fact that I am not a very funny person. In one particular situation, I was teaching a senior level time management course. The session had been very heavy and serious. I wanted desperately to "break the ice." A John Cleese film made them laugh and made me look very good. Thanks, John.

QUESTION RECORDING TECHNIQUE

Purpose

One of the major challenges for the trainer is how to handle questions. Trainee questions can be extremely valuable for enhancing learning, but they can also seriously impede the flow of a training course. Question Recording is the method I use to obtain the benefits of trainee questions without disruption.

Description

1. Set up a flip-chart at each side or at the back of the classroom.
2. Ask trainees to write their questions on the flip-charts, and these questions will be answered when a natural break in the course content occurs. Questions can be written at any time during the session. See Figure 7.
3. A variation on this technique is to ask trainees to record their questions on index cards, and collect these index cards from time to time.

Strengths and Weaknesses

Question Recording is an effective technique for remaining responsive to trainees' questions without suffering the negative consequences of answering questions during the session itself. Question Recording is also useful for the trainer, since questions are recorded in full view and serve as a form of feedback. However, the technique must be clearly explained to trainees, so that they do not get the wrong impression (especially the fact that you are not trying to discourage questions, only questions at disruptive times). However, if this is done, trainees will come to enjoy the technique and even be amused by having to get up and write questions on the flip-charts.* As an added bonus, Question Recording may also discourage stupid questions!!

In contemplating using this technique, one must be aware of the possible disruptive features of the technique itself. It is important

---

*For individual trainees who are reluctant to voice a question in front of a group, this technique may encourage them to silently write the question for subsequent review.

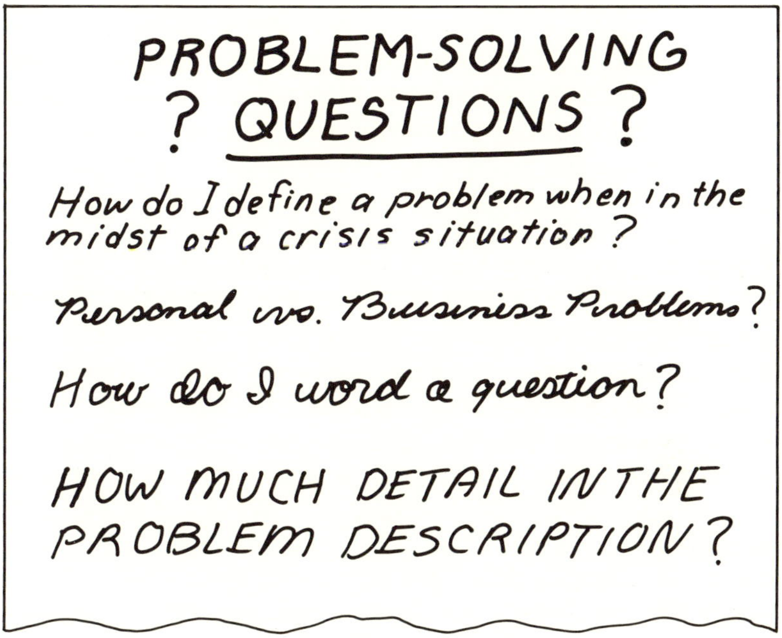

PROBLEM-SOLVING
? QUESTIONS ?

How do I define a problem when in the midst of a crisis situation?

Personal vs. Business Problems?

How do I word a question?

HOW MUCH DETAIL IN THE PROBLEM DESCRIPTION?

Figure 7. Question Recording.

that trainees understand how to use it. Depending on the layout of the room, it might be best to put the flip-charts at the back of the room (rather than at the sides). I like to place the charts at the sides of the room so that they will be in full view, but I will only do this if there is adequate room for trainees to reach the charts without interrupting the flow of the session.

Example

When I first started using this technique, I was looking for a way to keep trainees' constant questions from disrupting my training sessions. I have always understood the importance of trainee questions and encouraged them. Previously, my "need for approval" had dictated immediate response to every raised hand. I decided to ask trainees to write their questions down and ask them later. I found that they often failed to do so. Thus, I tried the flip chart approach to increase the likelihood that questions would be dealt with *at the appropriate time*. An informal evaluation of the situation (before and after) indicated that the quality of questions improved significantly, the number of questions decreased, and class disruption was markedly reduced. I now routinely use Question Recording in my training sessions.

PERSONAL VANTAGE POINT TECHNIQUE

Purpose

The purpose of the Personal Vantage Point is to encourage trainees to view course content in a more individualistic way. This will help trainees to become more personally involved in learning, and as a consequence, understand it better and retain it longer.

Description
1. Ask participants to review the course outline.
2. Ask them to decide on a certain "vantage point" from which they will look at the subject matter content. This might be some hypothetical person who is going to be called upon to structure and communicate the information to others in some unique way. This "vantage point" might be that of a newspaper or television reporter, a teacher preparing a lesson, or some other professional communicator of information.
3. You might describe possible roles briefly to the trainees, such as:
    a. Newspaper reporter: You are a newspaper reporter who is assigned to do an investigative report on .... (subject matter content).
    b. Teacher: You are a teacher who is trying to learn about .... (subject matter content) in order to teach it to a high school class.
4. You can develop a number of such scenarios and allow each trainee to select his or her own personal "vantage point."
5. Ask each trainee to try to assume this role position from time to time during the course.

Strengths and Weaknesses

This technique can be very effective at helping each trainee look at the course material in a fresh, creative and different way. This will enhance retention of information. It will also stimulate new ideas and insights. Taking a different "role" can free learners from their normal, rigid thought patterns, and release greater creative learning energy. However, in all such innovative techniques, there is always the possibility that trainees might view the exercise as "contrived." However, if you explain the value to such an approach, it will probably be well accepted. At the very least, many of the trainees will agree to try it, and benefit significantly from it.

Example

A training colleague has used Personal Vantage Point with considerable success in preparing for management succession. He would ask managers to assume their forthcoming positions as profit center heads in processing the information they were receiving. In another example, managers were asked to review product information from the "vantage point" of their competitors. The data that came from post-activity debriefing was so useful that it served as the basis of major marketing planning for new product development. Personal Vantage Point can be used effectively in any situation that demands "empathy" for another person's situation.

INVITING RECALL TECHNIQUE

Purpose

Inviting Recall is a method of self-suggestion that tends to create greater receptivity for remembering information. The technique identifies key points and then encourages trainees to remember them. It is an interesting adaptation of the "self-affirmation" technique discussed previously.

Description

1. When you reach a *key point* in the presentation, highlight it, emphasize it.
2. Invite trainees to recall the information, by saying something like: "This is a very important point for you to remember. I invite you to remember. Ask your memory to *invite this point in* and reserve a prominent place for it."
3. Ask trainees to take a moment and invite this key point into their memories.
4. Once you have done this, you can move on to the next course segment.

Strengths and Weaknesses

Inviting Recall is a simple, useful technique for increasing retention of important material. It requires only a brief pause in information presentation. This technique should be used only for key principles and information that must be memorized. Over-use of such a technique will dilute its effectiveness.

Example

One sales trainer reported that Inviting Recall has been a tremendously valuable enhancement to his training repertoire. "I ask trainees to invite recall at the beginning of the course and at the beginning of each major course segment. In addition, I find it most useful in facilitating the memorizing of appropriate responses to standard customer objections." This trainer reports remarkable improvements in objection response retention. He found that it cued trainees to know when a particularly important point was being raised and was worth remembering, provided emphasis for key concepts, and encouraged trainees to take more personal responsibility for retaining several response options for each standard objection (stimulus).

KEY CONCEPT RECORDING TECHNIQUE

Purpose

The purpose of Key Concept Recording is to reinforce and highlight important teaching points in a training course.

Organizing Information 61

Description
1. When you reach a particularly important point in the course material, write it down on a flip-chart page. Write all points in large letters so that everyone in the class can see each point clearly, without straining their eyes.
2. When each page is full, tape it somewhere around the classroom in full view of all trainees.
3. Continue this process throughout the course.
4. It is interesting to note, that if you end up with too many pages taped around the room, you probably have emphasized too many points! This is a good way to monitor your skills at iden- identifying truly *important* points.

Strengths and Weaknesses
Key Concept Recording is a very useful method of emphasizing really important points. It is also a helpful method of checking the trainer's natural tendency to emphasize too much. Be careful to highlight only the *key* concepts. There may also be a problem of not having enough wall space for other purposes. However, I think you will find Key Concept Recording to an extremely easy and graphic way to focus each trainee's attention on points that truly are *most important*.

Example
Many trainers particularly like this technique because it creates a very results-oriented environment. I have seen a number of trainers transform a drab classroom into a total learning environment through creative Key Concept Recording. The use of multi-colors has tended to enhance the effectiveness and value of this technique.

This technique is particularly useful when individual members of a team must each perform separate, but related, functions. The highlights recorded on flip-charts become personalized agendas for each individual. Because each participant needs to understand the role of his or her teammates, the page of highlights is of particular value to effective team functioning.

This use was demonstrated in a program involving a team of sales and service representatives for a large electronics company.

In this program, the recorded concepts provided each member of the team with the most important concepts to remember. As individual contributors to a group effort, this enabled the team to work with greater coordination back on the job.

ASSOCIATIVE THINKING TECHNIQUE

Purpose
The purpose of Associative Thinking is to provide trainees with a memory enhancement method for increasing retention of important information. This is but one of many memory enhancement methods that can be used.

Description
1. When you reach a point that you feel is vitally important for trainees to remember, ask them to select some object to associate with the point.
2. It is probably best for you to suggest that they choose an item with which they are intimately familiar, perhaps something around their house.
3. Ask trainees to spend a few minutes thinking about the association between the course point and the household object. You might stimulate their associative thinking by asking such questions as:
    a. What do the point and the object have in common?
    b. Why did you select the object you did?
    c. What is unique about the teaching point and what is memorable about the object.
4. Ask the trainees to spend a few minutes thinking of the point and the object together in their house (or wherever the familiar object happens to be).
5. This technique can be used to help trainees remember single points or lengthly lists.

Strengths and Weaknesses
Associative Thinking is a very effective way to assist people to remember points and lists that would otherwise be relatively

Organizing Information

meaningless to them. Association of an unfamiliar idea with a familiar one tends to greatly facilitate recall. However, the effective application of this technique might take some practice. There is always the possibility that a technique such as Associative Thinking might interrupt the flow of the course by becoming its own separate instructional unit. However, gaining experience in using the technique will minimize such problems. You will probably find that some people will have an easy time with this technique, while others might struggle in trying to find associations. This is always a potential problem in techniques that require personal creativity.

Example

Associative Thinking is being widely used in a company to assist manufacturing foremen to remember a critical sequence of production events. Trainers have become extremely adept in stimulating associations. Many foremen who once found the technique difficult are now using it frequently in their own self-learning activities.* *For example, foremen learn to associate a certain warning signal with an immediate response* (i.e., a series of short beeps with a partial system shutdown). This is important since, in emergency situations, foremen do not have a moment to spare. Associative Thinking has greatly shortened response time in critical situations, and, in one notable case, avoided a major leakage of a dangerous liquid.

*The technique is especially valuable when important, but very seldom used procedures need to be understood, retained and applied at a moment's notice.

CONCEPT EXAMPLES TECHNIQUE

Purpose

Much training knowledge is composed of concepts, or categories, which need to be remembered. Concept Examples is a method for assisting trainees in achieving a better understanding and retention of important concepts.

Description
1. Write the concept name on a flip-chart page.
2. Underneath the concept name, write a working definition of the concept.
3. Position two flip charts, side-by-side. On one list examples of the concept, and on the other list non-examples of it.
4. Continue this process until you feel that the trainees have a firm understanding of the concept.

Strengths and Weaknesses
Concept Examples is an effective technique for enhancing understanding and retention of key concepts. It helps to focus attention on important points, while also expanding understanding through use of examples and non-examples. This technique requires the trainer to have a strong personal understanding of each concept, because of the need to generate a significant number of examples and non-examples. Consequently, this technique can be both challenging and extremely valuable for the trainer, not just for the trainee.

Example
Concept Examples is used frequently in a food service products company where detailed product knowledge is viewed as particularly important. Sales reps must explain product applications to clients and respond appropriately to customer questions. This demands flawless understanding of certain key product applications, full retention, and the ability to generalize to newly encountered situations.

For example, in selling against competing vending equipment, a sales representative was able to obtain a large order by focusing on the concept of cleanliness. This was in the customer's interest and the sales rep recognized the opportunity. He itemized oversights in design which left the competing product exposed (in the customer's mind) to a variety of unhealthy bacteria. The sales rep concentrated on basic competitive advantages and applied them to the customer's "conceptual" concern.

Organizing Information 65

CONCEPT DIAGRAMMING TECHNIQUE

Purpose

Concept Diagramming provides a technique for graphically showing the relationships between subject matter concepts. In many training programs, so many concepts are presented that trainees tend to confuse them and fail to see conceptual relationships. Concept Diagramming is an effective response to these potential problems. It is especially valuable for trainees who learn best from graphic or visual explanations.

Description
1. As you touch on an important concept, list it on a flip-chart page.
2. When you have filled a flip-chart page, show how these concepts relate to one another. See, for example, Figure 8.
3. You can use any number of diagramming techniques, although I tend to use circles and arrows.
4. You can draw your diagrams on separate flip-chart sheets and tape them up around the room to further reinforce learning.

Strengths and Weaknesses

Concept Diagramming seeks to show trainees the relationships among concepts. As such, it leads to a deeper understanding of the concepts on the part of both the trainee and the trainer. Again, however, this technique challenges the trainer to develop a clear understanding of not only the major course concepts, but also their interrelationships. When trainees do understand conceptual relationships, they are much more likely to remember and be able to use the concepts in their work.

Example

In one Fortune 500 consumer products company, there was initial resistance to using Concept Diagramming. Trainers protested that they did not think that course concepts, although related, could be easily diagrammed. This caused a need for trainers to study and rethink their own information more carefully and work together to develop concept diagrams. This rethinking led to

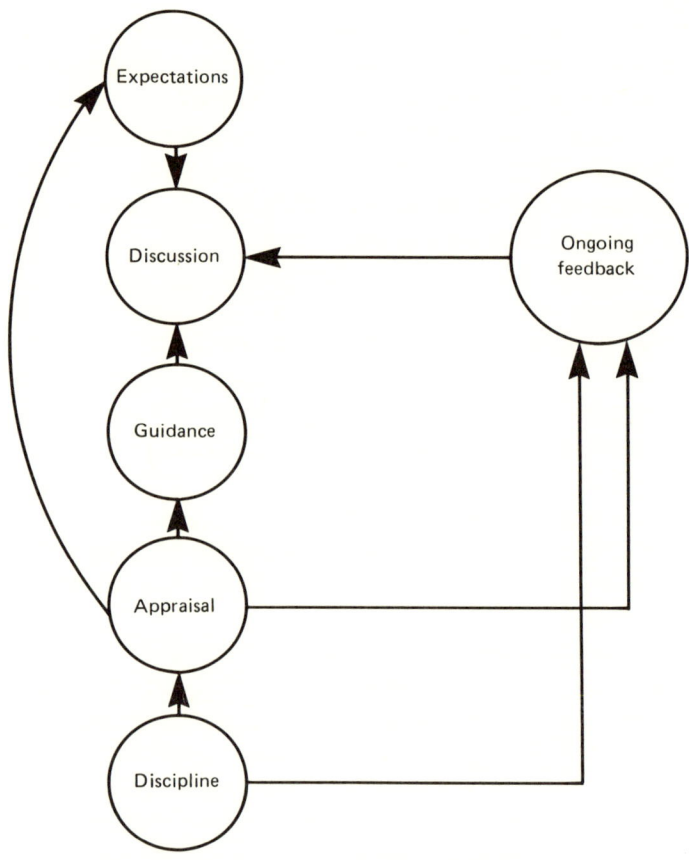

Figure 8. Concept Diagramming of Direct Supervision.

a better understanding of the firm's vertical markets and the key indicators used to forecast productivity. Performance and business concepts overlapped (as they always do), forcing the training group to become more proactive in understanding the strategies and policies which governed the activities of different work units.

METAPHOR TECHNIQUE

Purpose
The purpose of Metaphor is to assist trainees to achieve a more concrete understanding of previously abstract ideas. This technique provides trainees with familiar concepts to help them understand less familiar ones.

Description
1. Select a concrete metaphor (an example that is more familiar to trainees) for an important, but abstract concept which needs to be learned.
2. Explain to trainees how the metaphor is similar to the concept.
3. Illustrate the course concept and the metaphor on two side-by-side flip-chart sheets to demonstrate the relationship.

Strengths and Weaknesses
Metaphors are difficult to come up with, but when they can be found, they are powerful teaching tools. A good metaphor, like a good picture, is "worth a thousand words." The difficulty comes when the metaphor is not an appropriate one. Therefore, it is highly recommended that this technique be used selectively—only when there is a very clear metaphor that adds significantly to learner understanding.

Example
A government trainer I know was having a very difficult and frustrating time explaining telecommunications concepts to her trainees. As a subject matter expert, she understands these concepts well. It was a harrowing experience trying to explain them to non-technical trainees. She selected the metaphor of a river to illustrate the flow of information and the rapids to illustrate the effect of information entropy. Suddenly the lesson came alive to her trainees, and the previously arduous training task became much easier and more fun for all concerned.

PERIODIC SUMMARIZING TECHNIQUE

Purpose
The purpose of this technique is to provide regular summaries of information during the course to enhance understanding and retention of the material. It is amazing how often trainers pass over information and never return back to it, except perhaps at the very end of the course (during the final course summary). Using this technique will help trainers avoid this unhelpful tendency.

Description
1. Break the course subject matter into information modules. Limit these modules to no more than one hour in length.
2. Make sure that the information covered in each module is summarized when the end of the module is reached.
3. Alternatively, the trainer can make it a point to summarize subject matter covered every hour.

Strengths and Weaknesses
Periodic Summarizing is a simple technique which will focus the trainer's attention on the importance of regular summarizing of course material. Actually, such a device should not be necessary. It should be a routine instructional task. However, the fact that regular summarizing is so rarely done has necessitated the development of a technique to increase its likelihood.

Example
The training unit in a nuclear power plant was experiencing time crunch. More and more information needed to be learned in less and less time. In addition, the span of retention was particularly critical, due to the seriousness of the consequences in the workplace should information not be remembered. Periodic Summarizing provided an appropriate response to the challenge. Previously, trainers had tended to ramble on and on, without giving trainees a chance to consolidate their learning. The astute training manager realized that this situation had to change. By dividing information content into manageable "chunks," and scripting summaries for each chunk, trainers were better able to pace their presentation, and

make sure that key content elements were rehearsed. This allowed trainers to move quickly without sacrificing retention. The risk of failure was just too great to take any chances with incomplete learning.

CONCERT READING TECHNIQUE

Purpose

Concert Reading is a potentially powerful, if unorthodox, technique for increasing retention of course information. Originally reported in the "superlearning" literature of Lozanov and Barzakov, it is a training method of proven value. Few human activities exercise as many brain functions as playing and listening to music.

Description

1. Play some suitable background music. "Superlearning" proponents recommend Baroque piano music.
2. Ask trainees to read the material to be learned out loud, using *the same basic beat as the music*.
3. Repeat this process several more times.

Strengths and Weaknesses

Concert reading is effective. Some remarkable results have been reported when it has been used correctly. Scientists believe that internal cognitive maps may guide listeners to integrate or reject musical information. Concert Reading is most effective when there is a substantial amount of verbal material that needs to be remembered. The major weakness in the technique is that it must be done correctly to be truly effective. This requires someone who is familiar with the technique and also sensitive to subtleties of the Baroque musical background. Some practice is necessary, but the results can more than justify the effort. Also, you should be aware of the obvious fact that some people might view reading to music a little "weird"!

Example

Concert Reading has been used very effectively in teaching long lists and scripts. For example, a group of sales representatives in a large wholesale food distribution company were able to quickly memorize a sales script using this technique. This task would have probably taken at least twice as long without the use of Concert Reading, and it would not have been nearly as much fun!

Trainers using the technique report that the length of scripted material is not a critical variable, although 1-2 pages, double-spaced appears to be optimal. Two to three repetitions are also recommended.

REPETITION TECHNIQUE

Purpose

The purpose of Repetition is to highlight important points and to increase retention of key subject matter content. Although much less "artistic" than Concert Reading, it is easier to use, is probably less intimidating, and can be very effective.

Description

1. Stop when you reach a particularly important piece of information that you want trainees to remember.
2. Ask participants to repeat it after you or along with you.
3. Continue repeating the information until you are confident that it will be remembered.

Strengths and Weaknesses

Repetition is a very simple and effective instructional technique to use when remembering important information. It should not be used too often, and is most effective when the information to be learned is relatively brief. You will find that Repetition will also point out areas of subject matter that are most important so that trainees can focus on them. Some trainees might object to such a "rote" method, but if it is introduced properly and used with restraint, this should not be much of a problem.

Organizing Information

Example

Obviously it is not important for trainees to remember everything verbatim. But when memorizing is important, Repetition is a very simple way to achieve it. A colleague has used this technique for facilitating memory of essential concepts and their operational definitions. In one case, trainees needed to remember the function of a series of switches. The trainer asked trainees to repeat these functions over as they observed slides of the various distinctively color-coded switches. Several repetitions was all it took for these trainees to increase their retention of the switch-function association by 50 percent over individuals who had not engaged in the Repetition activity.

FILL IN THE BLANKS TECHNIQUE

Purpose

The purpose of this technique is to reduce the need for constant note-taking, while also obtaining the benefits that come from doing so. This way trainees can have notes, without having to exert so much effort taking down every word.

Description

1. Prepare a set of course notes for each trainee with blanks replacing many key words and thoughts. See Figure 9.
2. Ask trainees to fill in these blanks as the course progresses.
3. When you get to a point where it is appropriate to fill in a blank, advise trainees to do so.

Strengths and Weaknesses

Note-taking can be a very valuable learning tool. Unfortunately, it takes a lot of effort which could be better directed at other aspects of learning. Fill in the Blanks note-taking gives all trainees a standard set of notes, but allows them some active participation in completing them. This type of note-taking reduces the common problem of poor note-taking and still incorporates much of the value of doing so. One of the liabilities of this technique is that it requires extensive preparation to produce such a set of course notes.

The supervisor should ensure that subordinates have clear _expectations_, receive prompt, appropriate, and accurate _feedback_, and provides regular _coaching_ to improve work performance. Job descriptions are never an adequate way to ensure clear _expectations_ and annual performance appraisal is never an adequate substitute for regular _feedback_. Furthermore, training is not an adequate substitute for _coaching_ by the effective supervisor. And all of this should be done with a sense of dignity and _respect_ for the individual.

Figure 9. Fill in the Blanks.

Some also object to the "fill in the blank" format which resembles poorly written programmed instruction (which it is not intended to simulate).

Example

I learned this technique from a very effective management trainer while attending one of his leadership courses. This structured note-taking technique permitted my colleague to initiate frequent verbal exchanges with trainers or between trainees. At the same time, we all felt a certain amount of responsibility to return to the course notebook to make entries as directed. I found that this type of "structured" note-taking reduced the effort of note-taking without sacrificing the benefits. It encouraged trainees

Organizing Information

to listen for the "big picture," rather than getting "hung up" on writing down as many words as they could. I found that using this technique greatly increased my retention of the subject matter, focused my attention on what was really important, provided structured involvement, and required minimal effort. After the course, these "completed notes" served as a more valuable reference than the illegible scrawls I usually produce.

CATEGORIZATION OF NOTES TECHNIQUE

Purpose
The purpose of Categorization of Notes is to provide trainees with a structured opportunity to review their notes and actively work with them. As we all know, trainees often take notes during courses and seldom, if ever, look at them again. In fact, I have done this myself more times than I would like to admit! However, it is clear that notes can, and should, be a very effective learning and review tool.

Description
1. Encourage trainees to take notes any way they are comfortable doing so.
2. At regular intervals during the course, ask trainees to review their notes.
3. Give trainees approximately five category headings relating to the course subject matter. These should probably be the five key concepts in the course.
4. Ask trainees to write one or more of these concepts in red next to each note to which it applies.

Strengths and Weaknesses
In note-taking lies one of the great untapped resources for increasing learning. In order to tap this resource, trainees must begin to use it. Categorization of Notes is a simple technique for encouraging trainees to review their notes during the course, if not afterwards. This will reinforce the subject matter content, encourage more active learning, and increase retention of information. The

only negative is that using this technique can cause an interruption in the flow of the course. However, this potential problem can be overcome by scheduling reviews during normal breaks in the content.

Example

Categorization of Notes was my response to a personal frustration that came to a head during a course on Personal Computer Literacy. Trainees were taking copious notes, but I realized that these notes would be relatively meaningless to them, unless they were reviewed. I came up with the idea of asking them to categorize their notes *during the course itself*, rather than allow random recording of loosely related information which would probably never be read again. At several junctures in the program, I asked trainees to stop and review that section of their notes for about five minutes. Often, these brief reviews involved hands-on experience with related computer operations. I was frankly astounded by the positive response I received. Not only did trainees enjoy this opportunity to review their notes, but it also significantly increased retention on an end-of-course quiz, as compared with results from my previous running of the same course.

OBJECTIVE REVIEW TECHNIQUE

Purpose

The purpose of Objective Review is to repeatedly direct trainee attention to the course objectives. Too often objectives are presented at the beginning of the course and then ignored for the remainder of the training program. Objective Review will ensure this is not done, and will help to focus attention and increase retention.

Description
1. Periodically stop at a "natural" break in the subject matter content.
2. Review the course objective(s) relevant to that part of the subject matter with trainees.
3. Show how the content that has just been covered meshes with the objectives.

Organizing Information

Strengths and Weaknesses

Course objectives are often ignored once they have been presented. However, objectives can, and should, be an integral part of any instructional process. Objective Review provides a simple and easy method for continually bringing course objectives back to the consciousness of trainees. The price one pays for this is the need to stop and review. However, this small price will be rewarded amply by increased understanding and retention.

Example

It was a trainer with a prominent computer company that demonstrated the importance of this technique. He continually demonstrates in his training, the value of repeatedly returning to the original course objectives. In quite a technical curriculum of courses, it is easy to lose sight of performance requirements in favor of subject matter knowledge. By returning to the course objectives (stated, of course, in performance terms), this colleague was able to increase the likelihood that trainees would *focus on performance rather than information* in their learning. After all, in a work environment, of what value is information if it does not lead to improved performance? Objective Review helped trainees focus on the purpose for the course and reason for information. It helped them to organize subject matter content and improve the level of learning. Even with very technical subject matter, the trainer was able to use Objective Reviews to ensure that trainees never lost sight of course objectives and, consequently, rarely missed the forest for the trees!

GLOSSARY DEVELOPMENT TECHNIQUE

Purpose

Glossary Development is a technique to encourage trainees to remember key course concepts and their definitions. It also provides an opportunity to point out and highlight key points during the course.

Description

1. Prepare a blank glossary in the back of the trainees' course notebook. List the key terms and concepts with a blank space for the definition. See Figure 10.
2. As each of the terms or concepts is being discussed, ask trainees to turn to that term in the glossary and write in the definition.
3. A further variation on this technique might include asking trainees to write their own versions of the definition, rather than the definition given by the trainer.
4. A "hybrid" version of this technique might include some definitions that are already written out and some that trainees are asked to write themselves.

Strengths and Weaknesses

Glossary Development is a good way of encouraging trainees to remember (or at least gain increased familiarity with) important terms and concepts. Trainees will essentially write their own glossary as the course progresses. This reinforces key concepts, stimulates deeper understanding, and enhances retention. Obviously, this technique should not be used if familiarity with terms and their definitions is not important. It is not necessary to include all terms, as this exercise should be limited to those terms which are important for the trainees to remember. A risk is that some trainees will neglect to write down definitions, either because they think they already understand them or lack the motivation.

Example

A technical trainer was looking for a method of encouraging trainees to remember important terms and corresponding definitions in his courses on new equipment operation. He discovered this simple, but effective technique. The many trainers that now use it have found that this "personal glossary" is much more effective as a learning tool than a glossary that has already been prepared for trainees in advance. Even trainees who are relatively uneducated in a formal sense can still benefit by taking responsibility for writing (and thinking through) a few key definitions.

One of the added benefits of Glossary Development surfaced during a public seminar on local area networking. The presenter was

Organizing Information

Personal Glossary
MANAGEMENT CONCEPTS

Strategic planning	Long-term plans that focus on the identity of the organization.
Operational planning	Annual plans that provide a program of action for accomplishing objectives.
Decision-making	A systematic process for choosing between alternatives.
Organizing	Developing structures for managing.
Communication	Two-way flow of information between people.
Motivation	Stimulating people to act appropriately.
Training & Development	Activities aimed at improving employee job performance.
Problem-solving	Analyzing and identifying the best solutions for work problems.
Quality Control	Setting standards of quality and maintaining them.

Figure 10. Glossary Development.

---

using this technique with some very technical subject matter to respond to the trainee's interest in compiling complete and accurate definitions for all concepts. At various points in the seminar, course participants began reviewing each other's definitions before permitting the presenter to continue! The result was better understanding of the concepts on the part of participants and more active involvement in the program.

4

Practice for Retrieval

In this chapter, you will learn techniques for gaining the active involvement of trainees in learning. This active involvement will provide valuable opportunities for trainees to practice their knowledge and skills. As a consequence of this practice, trainees will be much more likely to be able to retrieve and use the information that has been stored in long-term memory, and use it appropriately. These techniques will assist you in:
1. Emphasizing the importance of on-the-job application.
2. Increasing trainee and supervisor commitment to action.
3. Stimulating critical and creative thinking.
4. Relating learning back to course objectives.
5. Adapting the curriculum to individual needs.
6. Providing simulated practice experiences.
7. Bridging the gap between the classroom and the job.

These techniques will further equip you to create more active, involving, and job-relevant learning experiences for trainees. The focus of this part of the book is the importance of never losing sight of the fact that the ultimate goal of training is not on learning or behavior but on improving on-the-job performance.

MULTI-PHASE PROGRAMMING TECHNIQUE

Purpose

The purpose of Multi-Phase Programming is to provide trainees with the opportunity to apply what they learn in training sessions to their work on the job. This is a method for increasing the relevance of training to the job.

Description
1. Break the training program into a number of modules.
2. Allow trainees to return to their jobs between course modules.
3. When they return to each training module, spend some time at the beginning obtaining information on how well trainees did in applying newly learned knowledge and skills to their jobs.

Strengths and Weaknesses
Multi-Phase Programming is an extremely valuable technique for aligning training more closely with trainees' jobs. When training does not allow for "return to work" breaks, it is often difficult for trainees to apply what they have learned. From the protected confines of the classroom, they are suddenly thrown into the "lion's den"! Multi-Phase Programming encourages gradual learning and gradual application.

Multi-Phase Programming is very difficult when trainees need to travel significant distances from their work to training. In such cases, it is costly and inefficient to allow trainees to return to and from training several times. Also, it may be necessary to sell the idea to management. However, when it is supported and logistically feasible, Multi-Phase Programming can have very positive effects on learning and on-the-job application. In addition, both trainees and trainers receive prompt, useful feedback on the effectiveness of the course.

Example
Multi-Phase Programming is most effective in teaching complex skills and when the duration of the course is longer than one week. In a ten-day customer service training course for a large retailer, trainees had been frustrated by their inability to "try out" their learning. In acquiring new skills for handling difficult customers, they needed to measure themselves in real work environments. Situational factors were so critical in measuring performance that no simulated role play would suffice. Once the skills had been tested, trainees wanted to regroup for self-appraisal and peer feedback. In response, the course was redesigned so that trainees would return to their jobs twice during the course. These "application periods" had a tremendously positive effect on the quality

of learning. Initially there had been resistance on the part of some trainees and many of their supervisors, who wanted to get the training "over with." However, once they witnessed the positive impact of the first application period, and recognized the improvements in handling problem accounts, they became strong supporters of the technique.

SUPERVISOR MEETINGS TECHNIQUE

Purpose
Supervisor Meetings are vital for maintaining a close and positive working relationship between trainees and their supervisors. Unfortunately, this relationship is often non-existent during training.

Description
1. Schedule at least one meeting between each trainee and his or her supervisor *during* the period of the training program.
2. Arrange for trainees and supervisors to discuss the progress of the course and relevant considerations for applying newly learned knowledge and skills to the job. You may even be able to tie course elements in with subsequent performance appraisals of newly learned knowledge and skills on the job.
3. Ask trainees to submit a brief resume of the meeting and their reactions to it. You might want to provide a simple form for this purpose. See Figure 11.

Strengths and Weaknesses
Supervisor Meetings provide a significant step towards integrating training and on-the-job performance. By scheduling at least one such meeting during each course, trainers are sending a strong message to supervisors, telling them not to "dump" their subordinates into the training program without adequate liaison. This will highlight the importance that should be placed on creating a meaningful bridge between the training and work situations.

Supervisor Meetings do sometimes pose a problem if training occurs in a central location and if supervisors are not truly committed to training results. Little can be done to overcome the loca-

```
                    SUPERVISOR MEETING LOG

    Date _____   Time _____      Subject _____

    Course Title _____

    Agreements:

    1. _____
    2. _____
    3. _____
    4. _____

    Follow-Up Actions
    1. _____
    2. _____
    3. _____
    4. _____

    Personal Reactions
    _____
    _____
    _____
    _____
```

Figure 11. Supervisor Meeting Log.

tion problem, but management support can go a long way towards overcoming supervisory resistance. When training is distant from the work location, you might consider telephone contacts during the course between trainees and their supervisors.

Example

A large trucking company was investing a great deal of money on maintenance training which was not paying off in adequate performance benefits. It became apparent to the consultant called in to study the situation that there was no mechanism for involving trainees and their supervisors in the training process. Trainees were returning to the trucking terminal and supervisors were totally ignorant of what had happened. It was as if the training had never occurred! Consequently, the new skills learned were soon extinguished, along with the motivation of trainees. It would be an understatement to say that training was being viewed as something of a joke. Supervisor Meetings were suggested as a remedial measure. Supervisors were trained in this new approach, which was fully backed by top management. Once this program was implemented, there were immediate and dramatic changes in learning and performance. This simple mechanism was able to create a "shared destiny" between trainee and supervisor that was previously missing. It turned out that the problem had not been due to deliberate resistance on the part of supervisors, only their ignorance of performance system dynamics. Supervisors were eager to play a more active role in employee development, especially when they saw that this development brought them performance based rewards. Specifically, improvements in vehicle maintenance led to reduced repairs per road mile and increases in the quarterly performance incentives awarded supervisors.

CASE STUDIES TECHNIQUE

Purpose

The purpose of Case Studies is to provide trainees with "realistic" situations with which to respond during the training program. Case Studies will provide an opportunity for trainees to try out their new skills prior to returning to the job.

Description

1. Prepare a number of realistic situation descriptions relating to the subject matter of the course.

2. Build into each situation an opportunity for trainee involvement. For instance, this involvement might include completing the case, responding to questions that follow the case description, or filling in blanks in the case study itself.
3. Ask participants to complete the exercise.
4. Discuss it with them.
5. This exercise can be done either individually or used as the basis of group discussion.
6. Three variations on this technique are:
   a. To develop two versions of the case: one a "best case" scenario, the other a "worst case" scenario (illustrating many of the problems that they might encounter on returning to the job).
   b. Use videotape "vignettes" to increase the realism of the case studies.
   c. Involve trainees themselves in the development of the case studies.

Strengths and Weaknesses

If cases are "too generic," they are unlikely to have the desired impact. Case studies should be developed by those who know the job well to maximize job-relevance and realism. The closer they are to real job situations, the more likely they will be accepted by trainees. When they are developed and used in this manner, they are likely to have a very positive impact on learning.

Example

A large telecommunications firm utilizes a three-day case study, including a detailed description of an entire community, competitive elements, cost parameters, etc. Top management teams form competitive units to work through the case from initial strategic planning to system implementation and evaluation.

Another organization uses brief videotaped situations to set the stage for case studies characterizing key customer service interaction situations. Trainees are asked to respond to these situations and are given feedback on their responses.

A very effective supervisory training program uses brief video vignette "mini-case studies" which set the stage for each situation covered in the course. Trainees are asked to view these 2-5 minute video segments and then indicate how they would respond if they were in a similar situation. Trainees learn to respond appropriately through continual active response to case study situations and prompt feedback concerning the possible consequences of their responses.

SIMULATION TECHNIQUE

Purpose
The purpose of Simulation is to provide trainees with realistic training situations which are as similar as possible to actual job situations. In such a simulated context, trainees are expected to respond as they would if they were on the job.

Description
1. Design a "simulated" situation similar to trainees' actual job.
2. Give trainees an opportunity to respond/participate.
3. Build in some feedback mechanism.
4. Optionally, you may follow the simulation with a class discussion.

Strengths and Weaknesses
A realistic, well-designed Simulation can be an extremely powerful training technique. It provides trainees with an opportunity to practice their new knowledge and skills in a classroom environment, but with many aspects similar to that of their work environment. A Simulation usually requires considerable design sophistication in order to make it sufficiently realistic. Not only must the situation be realistic, but so must the response options.

Example
Probably the best known simulations are those that are used to train airline pilots. These "flight simulators" are so realistic that a pilot needs very little actual flight time in an aircraft to become fully competent to fly it. Flight simulators are capable

Practice for Retrieval 85

of simulating virtually any in flight situation or problem, and pilots can respond precisely as they would in a real aircraft.

A less well-known simulation was conducted for military personnel during a recent international hostage crisis. Conditions were restructured to scale and rescue options were simulated.

NOTE-TAKING TECHNIQUE

Purpose

The purpose of Note-Taking is to provide a simple method for active learning and trainee involvement in the subject matter. There are many methods of Note-Taking, some of which are familiar, others not.

Description

1. Illustrate various methods of taking notes.
2. Ask trainees to select the method they prefer to use throughout the course. Popular types of note-taking include:
   a. Two-Column Note-Taking: One column for recording what is said during the course and another column for personal observations and applications.
   b. Note-Taking Tree: a Branching diagram that shows the relationship between elements of subject matter. The trunk of the tree might be the course objectives.
   c. Creative Note-Taking: Involves a combination of shapes, colors, lines, arrows, etc., to show the relationships among course content. Trainees are encouraged to be creative in the use of colors and design in order to make their note-taking personally attractive and easily understood when reviewed.
3. Take several opportunities to monitor trainee note-taking during the course and offer feedback and suggestions.
4. You can encourage trainees to use their notes, if you ask them to refer to their notes from time to time during the course. This way trainees will realize that notes are to be *used*, not just written!

Strengths and Weaknesses

Note-taking is a well-established learning approach and its value is beyond debate. However, the use of "creative" approaches to note-taking is still relatively new. Note-Taking should actively involve trainees in "restructuring" the subject matter to fit their own learning and application needs.

Learning new methods of Note-Taking may require practice, but this effort will pay off, not only in this course, but in future courses as well. It is important to stress to trainees that Note-Taking is largely futile if the notes are not *used*. After the course, notes can provide the trainer with extremely valuable feedback. I find it most interesting to observe whether my teaching is being received by trainees in the way that I intended. Notes are usually an accurate reflection of what is being received.

Example

Most trainers take it for granted that trainees will take notes and that these notes will enhance their learning. A trainer I know makes no such assumption. To this person, note-taking is an important learning activity that must be structured as carefully as any other activity in the course. Not only does this trainer introduce Note-Taking in his courses, but he also personally monitors trainees' notes to ensure that they are accurately receiving the content of the course. The notes of selected trainees are perused by the trainer at the end of each class session to see what they are recording (as a reflection of what is being learned). Based on this feedback, this creative trainer is able to better prepare for subsequent class sessions, and guide trainees to higher levels of learning and performance.

INDIVIDUAL BRAINSTORMING TECHNIQUE

Purpose

Individual Brainstorming is a method of encouraging creativity during training sessions. It is an individual version of group brainstorming.

Description
1. Pose a question or problem to trainees.
2. Ask them to generate as many solutions, answers, or ideas as they possibly can.
3. If appropriate, you might ask trainees to prioritize their lists.
4. In order to overcome the lack of "group synergy," you can provide trainees with a starter list of solutions or answers to stimulate their creativity. These sample ideas can be written on a flip-chart or provided as a hand-out.

Strengths and Weaknesses
Although Brainstorming is usually thought of as a group technique, there is no reason why it cannot be used individually as well. I often ask trainees to generate creative ideas throughout a course. Sometimes it is too time-consuming to break trainees up into groups. There are certainly advantages to group creativity, but this does not tend to be as important in learning situations as it is in actual on-the-job problem-solving.

Example
During some of my training courses, I stop from time to time to involve trainees in Individual Brainstorming. For example, when I am covering the subject of employee discipline, I might ask trainees to make a list of as many discipline methods as they can generate. Then, I might ask them to rank these methods in order of desirability. This quick and easy individual brainstorming is a good way to involve trainees in learning with a minimum of difficulty and very little expenditure of time.

BUMPER STICKERS TECHNIQUE

Purpose
The purpose of Bumper Stickers is to involve trainees in a fun activity, which will encourage greater understanding of the course content. This is a technique for quickly and easily livening up a course when the content might be getting a bit "dry."

Description
1. At the beginning of the course, explain to trainees that, at any time during the course, you might ask them to create "bumper stickers," or slogans which can successfully communicate course concepts to others.
2. Distribute large mailing labels to trainees for this purpose.
3. At appropriate points in the course, ask trainees to write a few Bumper Stickers and stick them on to a predetermined location in the training room.
4. A variation on this technique is one called "Graffiti," which is just like Bumper Stickers, but there are a number of flip-charts or boards around the room where trainees can be creative with their own graffiti relating to the course content.

Strengths and Weaknesses
In many courses, the presentation can become too serious, and some lighter activity might be in order. Bumper Stickers is an easy activity to add "life" to the class and briefly involve trainees in a creative activity which will contribute to greater understanding of the subject matter content. Only a few minutes need be spent on this activity, and it should rarely be repeated more than twice during the course. Otherwise, a change-of-pace technique will become "routine."

Example
I might be talking about communication skills with a group of supervisors. The lecture is getting a bit "heavy." I can sense the build-up of tension. Now is the time for Bumper Stickers. I ask trainees to take out their labels and create some Bumper Stickers which relate to the subject we have been talking about. We might get such slogans as:

"Do you know where your subordinates are today?"
"Speak softly but carry a long stick!"
"Work isn't school."
"Love your boss."
"I'm in training."

After they do this, paste the bumper stickers around the classroom during a ten-minute break (and have a chance to look at others' bumper stickers). At the beginning of the next session, I point out a few of the most creative Bumper Sticker slogans. Then we get back to work with renewed energy and motivation.

DEVELOPING ANALOGIES TECHNIQUE

Purpose
Developing Analogies can be a useful technique for encouraging trainees to creatively involve themselves in the course content. Often abstract concepts are difficult to grasp and remember. Developing Analogies helps trainees personalize course content and make it "their own."

Description
1. When a particularly important and difficult concept is reached, ask trainees to think up an "analogy" for it.
2. Analogies might include:
   a. Some familiar concrete concept which has some characteristics in common with the abstract concept under discussion (such as a computer with a library).
   b. Another abstract concept that is "analogous" to the concept being discussed (such as a disciplining a child with disciplining an employee).
   c. A symbolic analogy (such as a river with a certain communication process).
3. You might ask trainees to describe the analogy on paper or share it with the class.

Strengths and Weaknesses
Developing Analogies is a good way to get trainees' "creative juices" flowing. It can be done at any appropriate time in the course in a very few minutes. However, the success of the technique depends largely on the trainer's ability to introduce the technique and, of course, the creativity of the trainees in responding appropriately. Providing trainees with a few illustrative examples can speed the process along.

Example

A trainer for a large electronics company likes getting trainees to develop analogies for theoretical electronic concepts. He feels that this technique tends to increase trainees' creativity and their personal involvement in the subject matter. It is not unusual for him to stop the training session at any time to ask trainees for analogies of the concept that is being discussed. For instance, he might use analogies of swimming under-water to demonstrate the concept of resistance or on-off light bulbs as an analogy for binary logic.

This trainer finds Developing Analogies equally useful for management training as for technical training. Asked for an analogy to the "manage by the numbers" philosophy, one senior manager described the public's fascination with detailed baseball statistics. He described it as "pseudo-management," practiced by fans who second-guess coaches and team owners. Not only was the analogy amusing, but it did make a clear statement about our natural desire to quantify events and "keep score."

OBJECTIVE REWRITING TECHNIQUE

Purpose

The purpose of Objective Rewriting is to refocus trainees' attention back on the course objectives. It also encourages trainees to take personal ownership in the objectives and the course outcomes they describe. Another purpose is to obtain some interim feedback on how well the course is satisfying the specified objectives.

Description

1. When you have completed a course segment, ask trainees to review the objective(s) relating to that segment.
2. Ask trainees to rewrite the objective based on what they actually learned, not what was supposed to be learned.
3. If no changes in the objective are needed, then that is fine.
4. Ask for any feedback concerning course objectives and suggestions for course improvement.

Strengths and Weaknesses

This technique is very useful for briefly focusing trainee attention back on the course objectives, which are too often forgotten once the course activities get under way. Objective Rewriting can occur at virtually any point in the course, and this technique provides a quick and easy way to reinforce the objectives. It is also a useful "interim feedback" device that can provide trainers with very timely and useful information on how well the course is progressing. However, trainers should be confident that no major changes in the objectives will have to be made. Otherwise, this technique can lead to embarrassing results. Also, it is important for trainers to demonstrate a genuine interest in the feedback they receive.

Example

This technique has helped me personally to take objective writing more seriously. Prior to using Objective Rewriting, I found that I could read the course objectives out loud to trainees and then forget them totally for the rest of the course. Now that I use this technique regularly, I have found that the course objectives take on a new relevance and importance. In one course in which I used this technique, the trainees really took my objectives apart! Since then, I have been more careful.

Another useful by-product of Objective Rewriting is the implications it has for revising course content. When trainees restructure objectives, they send clear messages about subject matter and the way it was (or wasn't) covered.

SHOULDS, WANTS, WILLS TECHNIQUE

Purpose

Shoulds, Wants, Wills is a technique that can be extremely useful for getting trainees more actively involved in realistically planning for what they will do when they leave the training program.

Description

1. Hand out a sheet of paper with space for trainees to write their "shoulds," their "wants," and their "wills." See Figure 12.

SHOULDS	WANTS	WILLS
IMPROVE MEAN TIME TO REPAIR BY 20%	IMPROVE BY 50%	IMPROVE BY 35%
SERVICE 10 CLIENTS PER WEEK	SERVICE 15 CLIENTS PER WEEK	SERVICE 15 CLIENTS PER WEEK

Figure 12. Shoulds, Wants, and Will.

2. Explain what these categories mean:
   a. "Shoulds" are what trainees feel that they are being told they *should* do after the course.
   b. "Wants" are what they would *want* to do in this area after the course (if there were no constraints on their performance).
   c. "Wills" are what the trainees feel they *can do* after the course (given perceived constraints in the work environment).
3. Ask trainees to fill out the form.
4. Optionally, you can discuss the differences between the shoulds, wants, and wills with the trainees individually or in the class setting.
5. Another approach would be to collect the forms, and mention some of the more interesting responses to the class.

Strengths and Weaknesses

Shoulds, Wants, Wills is a good technique for actively involving trainees in planning for implementation of the new knowledge and skills they are learning in the course. The technique is very flexible and can be used at virtually any point in the course, and as often as desired. It is extremely simple and easy to use. The only caution is to expect some major "implementation obstacles" to be raised. This requires trainers to be diplomatic problem-solvers when running this activity. It is important to help trainees to understand the constraints that cause "shoulds," "wants," and (especially) "wills" to be vastly different from each other, without encouraging their frustration. This activity will also yield valuable data for learning about job-related constraints and will be useful in designing future courses.

Example

Trainers sometimes live in an "ivory tower" world, which is far from the harsh realities of the shop floor, or even the corporate board room. I have found that Shoulds, Wants, Wills is a very useful technique for bringing this divergence into the open and demonstrating to trainees my sensitivity to the difficulty of turning training theory into on-the-job performance practice. Often trainees make it clear that the "shoulds" presented in the course are vastly different from the "wills" to which trainees are prepared to commit themselves. For example, in a course on performance appraisal, managers emphasized in the activity that, although they knew that they *should* coach their subordinates more regularly than once each quarter, they were unlikely to do so under existing organizational constraints. On occasion, this technique has taught me many things about real-world performance that I did not know. It has helped me to appreciate the fact that when I am training, I am also learning.

TRAINEE TEACHING TECHNIQUE

Purpose

Few techniques are as powerful in involving trainees in the learning process as Trainee Teaching. As trainers, we know well that one of the best ways to learn something is to teach it to someone else.

Description

1. Identify subject matter segments that are suitable for Trainee Teaching.
2. Assign brief segments to individual trainees.
3. Provide trainees with some background information on that subject matter area.
4. Ask them to teach their segment in turn to the class.
5. Alternatively, you can ask trainees to share with the class areas of personal expertise that are related to the course content.

Strengths and Weaknesses

Trainee Teaching is not only valuable as a technique for involving trainees more actively in their own learning, but it also provides a change of pace from your own teaching and tends to increase trainee empathy for the role of the trainer. It is probably best to match trainees with subject matter areas with which they have some familiarity. There is always the danger that trainees might provide erroneous or incomplete information, so this activity must be monitored very carefully. If there is some problem, then simply correct it with sensitivity. Be sure to set strict time limitations on trainee presentations.

Example

An office products company uses Trainee Teaching in its introductory training sequence for new sales reps. Each participant is required to become the "expert" on a particular product and present a features/benefits lesson to the class. The presentations must be no longer than five minutes and can take *any* form—there are no limitations on creativity. Presentations are rated by the trainer (for content coverage and accuracy), the class (for effectiveness) and the presenter (all lessons are videotaped for self-assessment).

Practice for Retrieval 95

As you might expect, this technique virtually guarantees that each participant leaves the course thoroughly familiar with at least one product!

SCAVENGER HUNT TECHNIQUE

Purpose

We all know what a Scavenger Hunt is, but what does this have to do with training? An ingenious training technique uses the same basic methods to involve trainees in active self-learning. It is a very effective method for making self-instruction more fun.

Description

1. Develop a list of self-instructional teaching and learning resources in the subject matter area covered by the course. These might include:
   a. Reference books and articles
   b. Instructional audio and video tapes
   c. Materials from the work environment
   d. Documentation from vendors, government or other outside sources
2. Distribute the list to trainees.
3. Ask trainees to use as many of them as they can during a specified period of time. This activity can be run during the course itself or during breaks between course sessions. It can take place in the classroom or in the work setting.
4. You might give trainees a form on which to record their observations of each resource they use.
5. You can either rely on the "honor system" or provide trainees with some tool for monitoring whether they really used the resource or not.

Strengths and Weaknesses

Scavenger Hunt is a useful technique for adding involvement and variety to a training course. It provides a familiar model for trainees to follow and allows them an opportunity to take personal responsibility for their own learning. The success of the technique depends largely on the creativity of trainers in developing a satisfactory "menu" of resources and on the monitoring system. Most trainees will find this activity an enjoyable and refreshing change of pace from traditional training activities. If the Scavenger Hunt is going to be implemented on the job, between training sessions, the full cooperation of managers and supervisors is obviously a prerequisite.

Example

A trainer who works for a major West Coast financial institution likes to use the Scavenger Hunt technique to familiarize new hires with reference materials and forms used in the bank. Early in the course, trainees are to be given a Scavenger Hunt menu and asked to locate certain materials and forms, and then bring these things to the next class session. Using this technique on the job familiarizes trainees with the location of these resources and creates greater interest and motivation to learn about them than if these materials had simply been introduced in class by the trainer. It also signals to the new employees up front that they are expected to take personal responsibility for their own learning.

PERSONAL LEARNING JOURNAL TECHNIQUE

Purpose

The purpose of the Personal Learning Journal technique is to make trainees more aware of, and active in, the process of learning. It also provides trainees with a valuable personal resource that can be referred to after the course ends.

Description
1. Each trainee is supplied with a notebook labeled "Personal Learning Journal."
2. Trainees are advised that entries in this journal should differ from their ordinary notes. The purpose of the journal, it should be explained, is to record "personal observations about the training program," rather than factual information about the content.

3. Time can be set aside at intervals during the course for trainees to make entries in their Personal Learning Journals. Evenings and break periods are good times for making entries.

Strengths and Weaknesses

Training can often become a one-sided and impersonal experience. Lectures still tend to dominate the training scene. The Personal Learning Journal can provide trainees with an opportunity to become more involved in the learning process. It also provides an opportunity for trainees to get more "in touch" with their feelings about training (both positive and negative). Another benefit is that, with the trainees' cooperation, Personal Learning Journals can provide very valuable evaluation data for trainers.

Obviously, in any such technique, trainees might be reluctant to express their real feelings. It is important for the trainer to explain the importance of such an activity, and the importance of being honest. Reluctance to make entries in the journal, caused by laziness, can be overcome by encouraging trainees to be brief in their comments, However brief, regular comments can be extremely useful.

Example

In some courses, in which lectures are the predominant training methodology, the Personal Learning Journal can be a useful, relatively non-disruptive method of gaining trainee involvement. It has been used effectively in courses to encourage trainees to become more aware of the nature of the training process itself and how this is affecting them. Particularly in management training, these observations can be useful in assisting managers to become more sensitive to the ramifications of sending their own subordinates to training programs. The excerpt in Figure 13 was taken from a Personal Learning Journal produced by a trainee in a time management seminar. As this example shows, such comments are personal and can help trainees to troubleshoot their own performance problems.

```
PERSONAL LEARNING JOURNAL

Course: TIME MANAGEMENT; SESSION #1

①LEARNED THAT MY MAJOR TIME-WASTER IS
PROCRASTINATION!!
②NEED TO ATTACK FIRST PRIORITY EARLY IN
THE MORNING. NEED TO ATTACK FIRST...
③I DON'T PLAN IN ADVANCE!! NOT AS
WELL AS I SHOULD.
```

Figure 13. Personal Learning Journal.

GUIDED IMAGERY TECHNIQUE

Purpose
The purpose of Guided Imagery is to provide trainees with an opportunity to focus on the real-world context of what they are learning, without having to develop a simulation or leave the classroom.

Description
1. Ask trainees to close their eyes and relax. You might want to use a quick-relaxation technique (such as the ones suggested earlier in this book).

2. Ask trainees to imagine themselves using the skills that have just been covered in the course. If trainees are from the same work setting, you might want to visually describe that setting.
3. Verbally run trainees through the entire task, using visually stimulating vocabulary (especially words that connote sensory experiences such as sight, touch, and smell to enhance the "reality" of the situation being described).

Strengths and Weaknesses

Guided Imagery can be a quick and helpful technique for providing trainees with "vicarious practice" in a certain skill. This technique has been proven successful in bridging the gap between the artificial classroom setting and the on-the-job situation. However, Guided Imagery requires considerable descriptive skills on the part of the trainer. Poor descriptions can seriously impede the effectiveness of the technique. Nevertheless, with the right tone of voice and descriptive words, Guided Imagery can be a useful way to encourage trainees to think about on-the-job applications of their new knowledge and skills without having to leave the classroom. One should be aware of the difficulty in using this technique with "mixed groups" of trainees for whom there is more than one application of the skills being learned.

Example

One trainer I know is really sold on the value of Guided Imagery and has acquired considerable expertise in using it. One interesting application of the technique that this person has developed is to mentally guide trainees back to their work settings to consider possible problems in using what they have learned on the job. For instance, he will verbally guide trainees back to their jobs using a very realistic description. He will describe the use of a new technique (such as a new form of interviewing). Then, he will ask trainees to "foresee" the problems that they might have with clients in implementing the new method of interviewing. The descriptive technique that this trainer has mastered seems to stimulate a high degree of realism. This use of Guided Imagery often results in the development of innovative methods for overcoming these potential problems, and all this before trainees ever return to the job.

PROBLEM-SOLVING TECHNIQUE

Purpose

There is little doubt that the application of new knowledge and skills on the job is often complex and difficult. The purpose of Problem-Solving is to focus trainees' attention on identifying methods of overcoming perceived obstacles to applying new knowledge and skills on the job. This is an opportunity for trainees to respond positively to perceived problems by overcoming them, rather than becoming frustrated by them.

Description

The trainer's "bag of tools" is full of problem-solving techniques. I can hardly think of a trainer who doesn't know several of them. Virtually any problem-solving technique can be used here, if it can be adapted for individual use. I generally use the following technique:
1. Ask the trainees to describe the problem as clearly as possible.
2. Ask them to generate a list of possible solutions.
3. Ask trainees to develop a list of criteria that must be part of any feasible solution.
4. Ask them to "test" each solution against the specified solution criteria.
5. Ask the trainees to select the solution from their list that best fits the criteria.
6. Solutions can then be shared with the class.
7. Note that steps 1-5 can be accomplished individually, in small groups, or in the full class context.

Strengths and Weaknesses

We ordinarily think of Problem-Solving as a group technique, but it can also be effective as an individual one. Problem-Solving (whether individual or group) involves trainees in a creative process of adapting course content to their own job-relevant context. Individual Problem-Solving is probably more difficult than group problem-solving, since trainees receive less feedback as the process progresses. However, it has the advantage of requiring less time, while still actively involving trainees in the process.

Example

Sometimes I prefer using individual Problem-Solving to group problem-solving, especially when there are time constraints. I can still get trainees to creatively attack problems, without the necessity of breaking them into groups. For instance, I might want trainees in a customer service training course to consider difficult problems with complaining customers. In such a case, I might ask trainees to engage in individual Problem-Solving. The great advantage of using this technique in such a situation is that most of the on-the-job problem-solving with real customers is accomplished individually. Thus, through the use of this technique, trainees receive job-relevant practice in the kind of individual problem-solving that they would ordinarily encounter on the job.

QUALITY DOT TECHNIQUE

Purpose

You might have already picked up the "play on words," and figured out that the Quality Dot is an individual version of the popular "Quality Circle" concept. This technique is intended to involve individual trainees in developing new approaches to improving their work situations.

Description

1. Ask trainees to think about their jobs, especially in the context of what has already been discussed in the training course thus far.
2. Ask trainees to individually "brainstorm" ideas for how job quality might be improved. Make sure that you explain that brainstorming involves the production of a large quantity of ideas, and the importance of deferring judgment about them.
3. Ask trainees to rank the job improvement ideas in order of their feasibility.
4. Ask trainees to come up with a list of their "top five" ideas.
5. These ideas can be handed in to the trainer, or they can be shared with the class.

6. You might want to provide trainees with "prompts" that can help them to consider possible areas of improvement in their jobs, such as:
   a. Type of tasks
   b. Task procedures
   c. Work environment
   d. Work standards
   e. Tools and resources

Strengths and Weaknesses

Concern with the "quality" of work design is a relatively new bandwagon that everyone seems to be jumping on. I think it is a very positive emphasis. The Quality Dot technique can provide the trainer with an easy method of focusing trainee attention on job quality considerations. It is particularly useful to get trainees to "theoretically" apply newly learned principles and techniques to their jobs. Obviously, the Quality Dot has the weakness of not involving group interaction. However, it has the benefit of teaching trainees to be self-sufficient and to take personal responsibility for improving their own jobs.

Example

The Quality Dot technique is particularly useful in helping trainees who generally work alone to view their jobs more positively and creatively. When I was working in a government research institution, I found that lab technicians were often frustrated by poorly designed work procedures. These frustrations often surfaced in training courses. The Quality Dot enabled me to demonstrate to them that they had much more control over their environment than they realized. In the process, it helped to encourage and develop many exciting new ideas. For example, in one class alone, trainees were able to parlay the Quality Dot exercise into six strategies for streamlining critical work procedures which were ultimately incorporated into the institute's standard operating procedures. Quality Dot is not so much an opportunity to muse about how much better the work environment would be as it is a chance to do something (individually) to make it better.

POTENTIAL PROBLEM ANALYSIS TECHNIQUE

Purpose
The purpose of Potential Problem Analysis is to give trainees a structured opportunity to identify possible problems that might impede the application of newly learned skills on the job. See Figure 14.

Description
1. Ask trainees to identify as many "problems" as they can that might impede the application of a particular skill or technique in their work environment.
2. Ask trainees to rate each problem in terms of how likely they are to occur and to what extent each would hinder (threaten) the effective application of the skill or technique on the job. This could be done using two simple rating scales, such as the following:
   a. Likelihood: (3) very likely
                   (2) somewhat likely
                   (1) not likely

   b. Threat: (3) major threat
                   (2) some threat
                   (1) little or no threat
3. Ask trainees to multiply the "likelihood" by the "threat" ratings to reach a total score for each item.
4. Ask trainees to identify their "major problems," those with the highest problem scores.
5. Optionally, these "highest rated" problems can be shared with the class.
6. Possible solution strategies can also be suggested by the individual trainee, the trainer, or by other trainees.

Strengths and Weaknesses
Potential Problem Analysis is another method for assisting trainees to look more closely at the on-the-job ramifications of using what they have learned in the training course. It is a method for anticipating and preventing potential problems before they become

POTENTIAL PROBLEM ANALYSIS

Skill: DIAPER MACHINE TROUBLE SHOOTING

Problems	Likelihood	Threat
Complete machine breakdown (SCORE=3)	Not likely (1)	Major threat (3)
Incorrect information from operators (SCORE=6)	Somewhat likely (2)	Major threat (3)
Miscalibration (SCORE=6)	Very likely (3)	Some threat (2)

Figure 14. Potential Problem Analysis.

real problems. It helps trainees to become more proactive in planning to return to the job after training, and it encourages trainers to make training courses more job-relevant. Some complain that Potential Problem Analysis focuses too much on what can go wrong, rather than what can go right. However, as long as the emphasis is on successful application, this should not be a serious consideration.

Example

Potential Problem Analysis or some related activity has been a prominent part of many of my training programs. I believe that training is worthless unless trainees can use their new knowledge and skills on the job. I don't want them to be surprised

Practice for Retrieval 105

(and unduly frustrated) by the constraints that they are bound to find on the job. Potential Problem Analysis is particularly important when skills and techniques are being taught that are rather novel and have rarely if ever been used before in that work setting. In most cases, it is far better to be safe than sorry!

Consider this example. A training consultant I know had many experiences of coming into companies as an external trainer, teaching "wonderful" new skills, and finding out that nothing had come of the effort. He discovered that the reason was usually the unanticipated obstacles that trainees encountered when trying to use their new skills. He had used Potential Problem Analysis in his management consulting work, and decided to try it in his courses. Toward the end of each course, trainees would be asked to identify potential problems and develop solution strategies. These solutions usually involved some communication with management and elimination of constraints back in the workplace. Results indicated that when potential problems were identified and remedied up front, performance improvement was far more likely. When the trainee was forced to confront problems for the first time as they occurred in the workplace, the results were much less satisfactory.

PROBLEMS INTO OPPORTUNITIES TECHNIQUE

Purpose
There may be some who suggest that trainers spend too much time defining "problems" and focusing on the negative. Here is a technique that turns that around to focus on the positives.

Description
1. Collect some of the "problems," "constraints," and "obstacles" that may have been collected during the course thus far.
2. Ask trainees to divide a piece of paper into two columns. One column should be labeled "problems," the other column labeled "opportunities." You can also provide trainees with a form which has the columns already labeled.

3. Ask trainees to select a given number of the problems, and write them in the "problems" column. Advise trainees to leave sufficient space between items.
4. In the "opportunities" column, ask trainees to try to turn the problems into opportunities. For instance:

Problems	Opportunities
a. Lack of supervisor support	Supervisor takes a personal interest in the project
b. Lack of adequate procedures manual	New procedures manual developed
c. Lack of incentives to use new skills	Use of new skills rewarded

5. Optionally, these "opportunities" can be shared with other trainees.
6. These "opportunities" can be further clarified by developing more specific proposals for actually implementing the opportunity.

Strengths and Weaknesses

Problems into Opportunities can be a useful technique for focusing on the positive: the opportunities for improving the work environment as a result of training, rather than simply the reasons why training won't improve performance. This is not intended to be a futile exercise in "positive thinking" but a method for seeing the "other side" of implementation problems. Providing some good examples at the beginning of the activity can reduce the difficulty trainees might have in focusing on the positive side of the issue. We must recognize that it is usually easier to define problems than opportunities. That is what makes this technique so important.

Example

A successful management trainer uses Problems into Opportunities to give a positive lift to training programs that are focusing too much on problem identification. He confided in me his opinion that "it seems like management training today is basically a form of problem-solving... Heavy on the problems, light on the solving!" After developing a list of problems, he asks trainees to "turn them around" and restate them in terms of opportunities. As an example, a trainee identified his firm's mix of services as too diverse and the source of limited profitability. Restated as an opportunity, he described the firm's low margins as good reason to consolidate and return to its primary business.

VIDEO FEEDBACK TECHNIQUE

Purpose
One of the major obstacles to effective learning is lack of feedback. Feedback is very often the most important instructional variable in shaping competent performance. Video Feedback is a good technique for providing this feedback on an individual basis.

Description
1. Ask trainees to practice the skill or technique being taught in this segment of the course.
2. When trainees are confident of their ability, videotape one complete practice session.
3. Playback the videotape and provide a commentary on the quality of performance.
4. Playback can occur in a class or individual setting, depending on a variety of instructional and interpersonal considerations.
5. Written feedback can be provided on a checklist.

Strengths and Weaknesses
Video Feedback can be a powerful technique for giving information to trainees and shaping competent performance. However, any such technique must be used with sensitivity. Trainees may be reluctant to have their performance videotaped, especially if the videotapes will be shown to others. Trainers must exercise great sensitivity in their handling of this situation, balancing relevant instructional considerations with the desirability of confidentiality. One other note of caution: Be sure not to criticize the performance. Tell trainees what they did well and make suggestions for improvement in the future. Don't tell them what they did wrong.

This will be obvious from your other comments, and it need not be dwelt upon.

Example

Video Feedback is widely used for providing trainees with very practical information about the quality of their performance. I have used Video Feedback in a great many courses, ranging from supervisory training to customer service training to training in equipment operation. In one recent sales training course, a number of trainees found the videotape feedback so useful in shaping their selling technique that they requested additional Video Feedback sessions once the course was finished.

In another organization, a small surveillance camera was positioned in the corner of a seminar room during an actual seminar for pre-qualified customers. Following the seminar, presenters met to discuss their performance and audience reaction. Video Feedback is a powerful force in helping shape the behavior of all those who are receptive to the message. There are few people who are interested in personal performance improvement who do not appreciate the prompt, accurate, and appropriate feedback they receive using this technique.

ACTION PLANNING TECHNIQUE

Purpose

Action Planning is probably the most effective method available for building trainee commitment to applying newly learned knowledge and skills. It is the ultimate bridge between training theory and practice.

Description

1. Ask trainees to specify the actions they intend to take when they return to the job, based on what they have learned in the course.
2. Trainees should write these actions down on a sheet of paper or on a form provided by the trainer.
3. Some trainers might want trainees to also specify a target date for initiating each action. See Figure 15.

PERSONAL ACTION PLAN

Course: *Performance Diagnosis*
Goal: *Production!* Rewards *Bonus pay!*
(increase 10% 1st month) More time for quality control

Obstacles	Action Steps	Target Dates
To convince Chuck Jenkins to free up time and commit to the project.	Discuss course with Chuck Jenkins and explain his role as my supervisor.	10/23
Employees may see it as extra work for no additional reward.	Meet with staff to discuss need for job aids.	10/25

Figure 15. Personal Action Plan.

4. I always recommend that the first Action Plan item always be: "Discuss this course with my supervisor within one week of returning to the job."
5. Action Planning can be done at the end of the course or after each segment of the course.

Strengths and Weaknesses

Action Planning is a powerful, yet simple, technique for gaining concrete commitment to action. Obviously, even this technique has its limitations. For instance, trainees may forget, or ignore, their commitments. However, while appreciating the limitations of all training techniques for impacting on-the-job performance, Action Planning is still one of the most powerful. One important suggestion bears stating: Encourage trainees to be *specific* in their action commitments.

Example

I use Action Planning in *every* course I teach. When the course is relatively brief, I ask trainees to complete one Action Plan at the end. When the course is long and complex, I generally ask trainees to complete an Action Plan after each course module. In order to further emphasize the importance of Action Planning, I emphasize the futility of the course if the Action Plan items are not implemented.

Working with an overseas government agency, I discovered that trainees already possessed the skills they were being taught. The unit manager could not understand why trainees did not use the skills if they already knew them. Using Action Plans to upgrade personal commitment, we verified existing competencies and pinpointed inequities in the reward system. As a result, an incentive plan was introduced, training dollars were saved, improved training options were made available, and employees began to demonstrate their real abilities on the job.

5

Evaluation of Learning

In this chapter, you will be exposed to many techniques for evaluating the amount and quality of learning that is occurring. This will enable you to better:
1. Adapt the course to the individual needs of trainees.
2. Make mid-course corrections if necessary.
3. Obtain regular trainee feedback.
4. Demonstrate your responsiveness to this feedback.
5. Assess learning during and after training.
6. Obtain information that will facilitate improvement of training courses in the future.

Nothing separates the effective trainer from the ineffective one more than *concern for improvement*. The techniques you will discover in this part of the book will provide you with powerful tools for obtaining trainee feedback and acting upon that feedback to maximize learning and performance.

FEEDBACK CARDS TECHNIQUE

Purpose

The purpose of Feedback Cards is to give ongoing feedback to trainers during the course. It is a simple and fun method of demonstrating to the trainees that trainers are doing their best to be responsive to their needs. It also adds a sense of humor to the course.

Description
1. Pass out to each trainee a set of color-coded feedback cards. On each card is a message, such as:
   a. Too fast!
   b. Information overload!
   c. Explain that point, please!
   d. Great point!
2. Ask trainees to display the appropriate card when they feel it is appropriate.
3. This way trainees will be more involved and trainers will receive immediate feedback on how they are doing.

Strengths and Weaknesses

Feedback Cards is a technique that can add a great deal of life to a course, especially at the beginning. You will find that the Feedback Cards will be widely used during the first few hours of the course, and gradually the novelty will wear off. But the beginning of the course is most crucial for both trainers and trainees. Feedback Cards will set a positive and responsive tone for the course and will help the trainer to adapt his or her teaching style to the needs of the group. Feedback Cards do require some investment and preparation time. Some may doubt the payoff for all this work. However, you should be aware that the cards can be used again in other courses. There is also the possibility that some trainers might be threatened by this technique. It does require an open mind and considerable humor. A few conservative trainers might view this technique as a bit "far out," but it works!

Example

I have used Feedback Cards in several recent courses. I have received nothing but positive reaction. I have found that it helps me to "get in touch" with my audience. Trainees find the technique to be a good "ice breaker" at the beginning of the course. And, just like the assembly line stop button that is never pressed, even if they aren't used, they give the trainees a sense of importance and control. I have gotten some good laughs by including a few really goofy cards, such as "Help!" "I need to go to the bathroom!" and "Coffee break time!" At any rate, Feedback Cards are harmless fun that can provide trainers with valuable feedback during the early stages of the course when "fine tuning" may be important.

FLIP-CHART FEEDBACK TECHNIQUE

Purpose
Flip-Chart Feedback enables trainers to collect ongoing evaluation data about the course. It also encourages trainees to think of evaluation as a useful, friendly, enjoyable, and ongoing activity, rather than a threatening one.

Description
1. Place one or more flip-charts at the side(s) of the classroom.
2. Ask trainees to write comments about the training program on the flip-chart at any time during the course.
3. Trainers should review comments at regular intervals during the course, and discuss key comments with trainees.
4. Trainers should collect feedback pages at the end of the course. These sheets will serve as a useful adjunct to data obtained through other course evaluation activities.

Strengths and Weaknesses
Flip-Chart Feedback is an extremely useful evaluation method. It is possibly the best method for obtaining interim feedback during the course because it does so with virtually no intrusion into other course activities; it collects information continuously; and it tends to make evaluation seem like fun. Obviously, there is always the risk that trainees will be intimidated by the public nature of this feedback-giving. However, it is up to the trainer to set an appropriate, non-threatening tone for this type of data collection to really succeed. When a positive atmosphere is created early in the course, it will permeate the rest of the program. As with Question Recording (described in an earlier section of this book), there is always the possibility that Flip-Chart Feedback could be a disruptive influence in the classroom. From my experience, this is rarely the case with mature adults who tend to understand the place for humor and the time for seriousness.

Example

I have used Flip-Chart Feedback with great success in many of my training programs. I have found that trainees may initially be reluctant to contribute comments, but, with a little coaxing, this technique becomes a kind of game. In an Introduction to Management course in which feedback had been historically poor, this technique was successful in "opening up" trainees and contributing to a much more positive relationship with trainers. I have had to prepare myself for comments that sometimes hurt, and often surprise me (and catch me off guard). It is precisely this kind of responsiveness that leads to improvement in trainer performance.

QUIZZING TECHNIQUE

Purpose

Quizzing is a technique for assisting trainers to monitor learning during a training course. Unfortunately, almost all evaluation is done at the tail-end of a course, and this significantly reduces the practical value of the data acquired. The purpose of Quizzing is to assess the quality of the training, not the performance of trainees.

Description

1. Prepare a series of brief "quizzes" on major modules in the course. These ought to be as practical as possible, and limited to one or two questions. Each Quizzing session should take no more than five minutes.
2. Explain to trainees that the purpose of Quizzing is to continuously assess the success of the training, not the performance of trainees. Quizzing is generally done anonymously.
3. Administer quizzes at the end of each major subject matter unit.
4. Collect and review the results at the next break in the course.

Strengths and Weaknesses

Quizzing is a valuable method of obtaining regular evaluation information about how much trainees are learning. Quizzing provides trainers with information when they can use it, during the course, rather than after it is over. Whether we like it or not, it is a fact of life that many people fear "tests." Quizzes, even short anonymous ones, may not be a popular innovation. However, if this activity is approached positively, and it is made clear to trainees that it is the trainer (and not the trainees) who is being assessed, this problem can be rather easily overcome.

Example
Quizzing is used by trainers in a large pharmaceutical company to measure the ability of sales trainees to distinguish subtle but significant differences in prescription drugs. These drugs are distributed to practicing doctors on a trial basis. The amount of time available for selling is severely limited, so it is essential that the sales representative be able to recognize "hot buttons" and immediately identify features and benefits. As part of an ongoing training effort, quizzing is conducted without notice on a regular basis. Product updates are frequent and the 2-3 question quiz is a way to help pinpoint new sales reps who are best prepared for added responsibility.

HAPPINESS INDEX TECHNIQUE

Purpose
The Happiness Index, or attitude survey, is the workhorse of training course evaluation. We often refer to it in a derogatory way, but it is hard to deny its value when used as part of an overall evaluation strategy. When all is said and done, the Happiness Index, in all its variety and formats, is still a very effective evaluation technique.

Description
1. Develop evaluation questions/items that reflect various dimensions of trainee satisfaction with the training program and will capture suggestions for improvement.
2. Use appropriate response scales, such as:
   a. True/false
   b. Agree/disagree
   c. Satisfied/dissatisfied

d. Interesting/dull
e. Lively/dry

Note that by using different response scales for different items, you will reduce the likelihood that trainees will give the same response to each item. Scales can be two-point, three-point, five-point, or seven-point.
3. Incorporate at least a few "open-ended" items.
4. Administer the Happiness Index.
5. Carefully study the information obtained.

Strengths and Weaknesses

The Happiness Index is a very useful device for obtaining evaluation data at the end of a training course. It is a relatively non-threatening instrument that both trainers and trainees are used to and comfortable with. Obviously, the design of the survey is the most crucial factor in its success. Some organizations use standard surveys, others devise surveys for each individual course. My suggestion is to get an expert to develop a good "generic" Happiness Index and use it for all courses. This will facilitate course comparisons.

The major weaknesses of the Happiness Index technique lies in two areas: (1) how it is designed, and (2) how it is introduced. Survey design is largely a function of the expertise of the designer. But implementation is a factor that can either enhance any survey or greatly detract from it. Too often the Happiness Index is thrown at trainees right at the end of the course, when everybody wants to go home, and few instructions are given. The success of the Happiness Index depends, to a large extent, on when it is administered to trainees and how serious the trainer appears to be about receiving and using honest feedback.

Example

I used to bad-mouth the Happiness Index until I witnessed the value of this technique when it is well used. A trainer for a major transportation company showed me how it should be used. First of all, the evaluation form has been carefully designed and is very short (rarely exceeding one page). He always distributes the survey prior to the last activity of the course. This way the Happiness

Index becomes a part of the training program itself, and not a last-minute after-thought. He also explains the purpose of the Happiness Index, and uses it as a public relations tool. He stresses the importance of obtaining accurate, honest, and complete data. Trainee response has been extremely positive to this approach, and the information obtained has been remarkably useful compared to most Happiness Indexes I have seen. This trainer has also reported that trainees are becoming increasingly more sophisticated in course evaluation as they attend additional courses. It is apparent that the success of the Happiness Index depends more upon its timing and method of introduction than even its design.

TRAINEE-DEVELOPED EVALUATION TECHNIQUE

Purpose
The purpose of Trainee-Developed Evaluation is a quick and easy method of gaining greater trainee involvement in the evaluation process. This technique will not only yield better evaluation data, but it will also provide trainees with a valuable learning experience.

Description
1. Distribute blank index cards to all trainees.
2. Ask each trainee to put him or herself in the position of the course trainer.
3. From this vantage point, each trainee should write one question that he or she would like answered about the quality of the course.
4. Use this information to design a course evaluation instrument.

Strengths and Weaknesses
Too often trainees remain passive "pawns" in the training process. They are "acted upon," and fail to become partners in the training process. In no aspect of training is this more true than in evaluation. I have found it extremely useful to incorporate trainee-developed items on course evaluation questionnaires. Not only do trainees often come up with good items, but, as a result of their

participation, they also take the course evaluation process much more "personally" and seriously.

You might want to incorporate some of your own items together with those developed by trainees. You can also edit trainee-developed items and use your own response scales. There are many "compromise" versions of this technique. However, any weaknesses in trainee-developed items are usually compensated for by the positive effects of trainee involvement in the process. It might be useful to provide trainees with a model before asking them to develop their own items.

Example

One organization uses Trainee-Developed Evaluation as part of its overall course evaluation strategy. Trainee-developed items are added on to a "generic" questionnaire to gain greater trainee involvement and to personalize it. Using this approach has contributed to a more positive trainee attitude toward evaluation, as well as an improved quality of evaluation data. Initially, completely trainee-developed questionnaires were tried, but it was found that this approach failed to explore some important aspects of training to which trainees were not attuned. The "compromise approach" has appeared to work better for everyone concerned.

EVALUATION INDICATOR IDENTIFICATION TECHNIQUE

Purpose

The purpose of Evaluation Indicator Identification is threefold. It involves trainees in an active process of identifying their own on-the-job evaluation criteria. It commits trainees to the evaluation process. It provides trainers with extremely useful information to help in designing more meaningful evaluation activities and instruments.

Description

1. Ask each trainee to make a list of aspects of work performance that might be affected by what has been learned in the training program.

2. Ask trainees to rank these aspects in order of how closely related they might be to what they have learned.
3. Ask them to suggest methods for assessing performance in these "indicator areas."
4. You might want to prepare a form for this purpose, with three columns labeled: "rank," "indicator area," and "measure." See Figure 16.

Strengths and Weaknesses

There is probably not another area of training that is so frequently ignored and poorly implemented as evaluation. One of the major problems is that trainers know so little about how to assess job-relevant performance. Oddly enough, we rarely go to the "experts" in the subject: the employees themselves. Evaluation Indicator Identification is a method for making use of trainee expertise, while also increasing their commitment to making the evaluation successful.

In all evaluation activities, it is crucial to stress that the primary purpose of course evaluation is not to evaluate individual trainees, but is for the purpose of course improvement. When trainees recognize their important role in this task, they are generally cooperative. You will be amazed by how much the trainees themselves already know about evaluation!

Example

I was contacted by a large industrial equipment manufacturing company to assist them in developing more "job-relevant" course evaluation methods. They wanted to go beyond the traditional "happiness index" to more sophisticated forms of on-the-job evaluation. Unfortunately, they knew very little about what to assess on the job. Evaluation Indicator Identification was the method that I suggested for determining what and where to evaluate. A trial of this method confirmed its efficacy. Trainees developed a list of indicator areas (such as "unit production" and "paint adherence") for each major job. Measures (such as "number of units produced" and "number of rejects") were developed for each indicator area. These performance measures were then monitored before and after the completion of each training program. As a re-

JOB EVALUATION

Job: Field Service Technician

Rank	Indicator Area	Measure
3	SPEED	MEAN TIME FOR REPAIR
2	CUSTOMER SATISFACTION	NUMBER OF COMPLAINTS PER WEEK
1	REPAIR SUCCESS	TIME BETWEEN CALLS FOR GIVEN PROBLEMS

Figure 16. Evaluation Indicator Identification.

sult, trainees felt much more involved in the evaluation process, were more committed to it, and the evaluation data obtained was of a much higher quality than it had been previously.

BEFORE AND AFTER TECHNIQUE

Purpose

The purpose of Before and After is to give trainees an opportunity to explore the changes that they have observed in themselves as a result of having attended the course. It also provides a valuable time for self-assessment and personal reflection. See Figure 17.

Evaluation of Learning 121

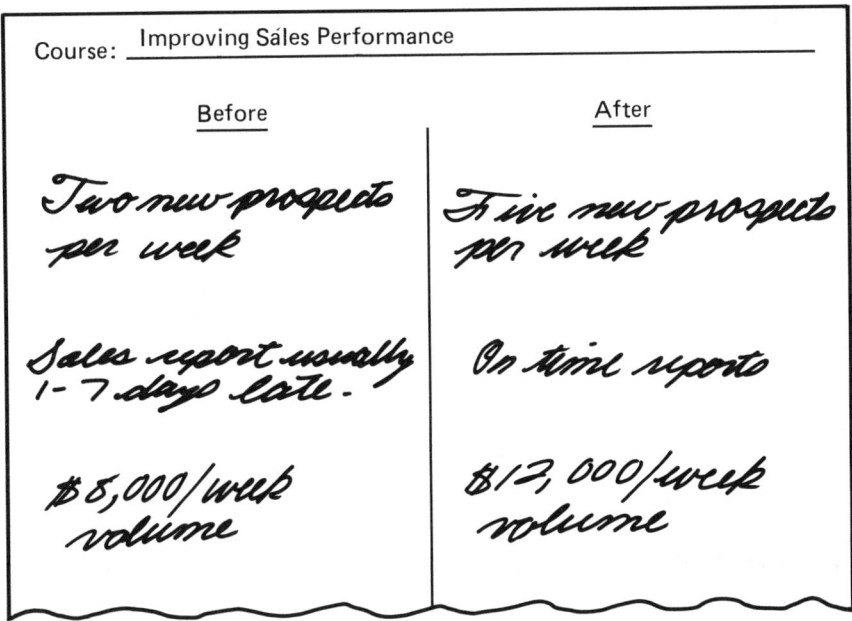

Figure 17. Before and After Form.

Description
1. Ask trainees to spend about five minutes reflecting on the course and how it has affected them.
2. Ask trainees to describe their capabilities before and after the training program. You might want to provide them with a form divided into two sections for their observations before and after training.
3. This can be used to identify *perceived* capabilities at the end of the course or *actual* capabilities if it is used when trainees have returned to the job.

Strengths and Weaknesses
Before and After is a novel approach to trainee self-assessment. It provides an opportunity for trainees to give some preliminary

indication of the changes (both personal and in terms of their performance) that they have perceived as a result of the training course. Some trainees might find such prediction of performance difficult. It is probably not advantageous to force trainees into responding. You might advise trainees that, if they are having difficulty in completing this activity, to simply write some comments about how the training program might be improved in the future.

Example

After experimenting with a great many evaluation techniques, a trainer with a government agency has found Before and After among the most useful. She uses the Before and After technique just before action planning. She finds that it gives trainees a chance to mentally review the course and assess personal impact. For example, one trainee observed the following: "Before: My subordinates would usually get upset when I had to give a negative performance rating. After: I now know how to defuse and redirect negative reactions, and I feel confident that I will be able to apply this in future performance appraisal situations." This technique can be viewed as a "warm up" to action planning, and it provides trainees with a useful time of self-assessment prior to making action commitments. She often selects Before and After observations for inclusion in evaluation reports and then contrasts these predictions with actual productivity increases.

BENEFITS AND COSTS TECHNIQUE

Purpose

Benefits and Costs is an interesting way of obtaining information about both the "pluses" and "minuses" of the training program. It is also useful in assisting trainees to assess both sides of the training experience.

Description
1. Provide each trainee with a two-column form with a heading for "benefits" and one for "costs." See Figure 18.
2. Ask trainees to list as many benefits of the training program as they can.

QUALITY ASSURANCE COURSE	
Benefits	Costs
① More confident with QA procedures. ② Understand Corporate policy. ③ Expect defect rate to decrease.	① Time away from job. ② New ideas require effort to implement. ③ Financial constraints. ④ Missed appointments ⑤ Added cost of temporary replacement worker.

Figure 18. Benefit/Cost Form.

3. Then, ask trainees to list as many costs of the training program as they can identify. These are not necessarily dollar costs, but can involve time, extra effort, customer response, material resources, etc.
4. Encourage trainees to respond in any way they wish. Do not place any restrictions on their responses.

Strengths and Weaknesses

Benefits and Costs is a quick and easy method for assessing some of the major pros and cons of the training program. It encourages trainees to consider both the positive and negative aspects of the program, and to balance them against one another.

This approach has some major advantages over more structured and complicated methods of evaluation. It avoids the threat of "leading questions," and allows trainees to respond in any way they see fit. This format has the disadvantage of possibly not providing enough structure for some respondents.

Example

In seeking a middle ground between too much structure and no structure at all, a colleague of mine who works with a small service organization discovered the value of Benefits and Costs. She has used this technique effectively for many of her end-of-course evaluations. By introducing the Benefits and Costs form with a minimum of explanation, my colleague has found that her trainees respond openly and creatively to the challenge. Using Benefits and Costs, she now feels that the positives and negatives of the course get equal emphasis, which is just the type of feedback she wants to receive.

CARD SORTING TECHNIQUE

Purpose

Card Sorting is another unusual, but effective course evaluation technique. It provides considerably more structure, and yet greater response options, than most other techniques as a way of obtaining higher quality evaluation information.

Description

1. Distribute a pack of index cards and a response form to each trainee. See Figure 19.
2. On each index card is printed a descriptive word or phrase (such as interesting, outstanding, enthusiastic, appropriate, relevant, dull, slow, uncomfortable) and a unique number.
3. The response form includes a number of course dimensions (instructor, content, class setting, instructional methods, etc.), each one followed by a blank space.
4. For each course dimension on the response form, ask each trainee to sort through the cards and select the descriptive word that best describes his or her reaction to that aspect of the course.

Evaluation of Learning 125

COURSE DIMENSION	YOUR RESPONSE
Instructor Enthusiasm	Luke Warm
Course Coverage	Complete
Job Relevance	Highly Relevant

Figure 19. Response Form.

5. Trainees should record the most descriptive word(s) or phrases(s) for that course dimension in the appropriate space on the response form.
6. Trainees should continue this process until the response form is completed.

Strengths and Weaknesses

Card Sorting is a rather elaborate method of training evaluation, but it does yield very good results. The reason for its effectiveness is that it is highly structured, but exposes the trainee to a wide range of response options. In most evaluations, there is only one rating scale on which to respond, with a very limited number of choices. In Card Sorting, there is a very large variety of options, which will generally increase the validity of responses. However, developing card sets is a more difficult and costly task than preparing a more conventional evaluation. Card Sorting also tends to take a longer period of time for the trainee to complete. A trainer, in deciding whether to use this technique, inevitably must choose between time versus quality trade-offs.

Example

A trainer for a financial services company uses Card Sorting for a very specific reason, to educate his trainees about evaluation. For many years he was frustrated by the superficial evaluation responses he received on traditional evaluation surveys. The problem was perceived to be largely one of lack of sophistication on the part of the trainees. But how could trainees be expected to adequately describe their training experiences without first learning how to do so? Card Sorting was seen as a way of increasing evaluation knowledge, in order to obtain more thoughtful and sophisticated responses. Card Sorting has turned out to be a highly effective educational technique, as well as an evaluation technique. Trainees who have participated in the Card Sorting activity several times are now able to respond much more appropriately in other evaluation situations as well.

TRAINEE-SUPERVISOR EVALUATION MEETING TECHNIQUE

Purpose

As I have indicated a number of times in this book, the relationship between the employee and the supervisor is perhaps the most critical one in the entire work environment. The purpose of the Trainee-Supervisor Evaluation Meeting is to provide an opportunity for the trainee and his/her supervisor to discuss the results of the training process and to plan for on-the-job application of the newly learned knowledge and skills. This is part of a continuing effort to sensitize both the trainee and the supervisor to the need for the closest possible working relationship.

Description

1. A formal appointment is made for each trainee and his or her supervisor to get together for an Evaluation Meeting. This meet-

Evaluation of Learning

ing should occur as soon as possible after the training course has been completed.
2. The supervisor (who has preferably been coached on how to lead such a meeting) should find out as much as possible about the program and the knowledge and skills the trainee acquired.
3. The supervisor should also discuss how the trainee proposes to use the new knowledge and skills in the job and what support and resources he or she might require.
4. The trainee and supervisor should also discuss the trainee's observations regarding the quality of the course.
5. The meeting should end with an agreement (preferably documented in writing) about what the trainee is expected to do on the job as a result of having taken part in the training program.

Strengths and Weaknesses

The Trainee-Supervisor Evaluation Meeting represents a very important step towards encouraging supervisors to take more personal responsibility for the training of their subordinates. Although few supervisors are actively involved in training programs, they ought to be actively involved before and after training. Otherwise it is difficult to translate learning into improved performance. Supervisors are often the key to employee performance, and any "meeting of the minds" between trainee and supervisor is bound to be a positive factor in the performance improvement process. The major weakness of any such technique is that it depends on the complete cooperation of the individual supervisor. In some cases, this may be a stumbling block to successfully implementing this technique.

Example

I would scarcely consider running a training program without encouraging the use of Trainee-Supervisor Evaluation Meetings. They are that important. In order to increase the probability that they occur and run smoothly, I generally organize "supervisor briefings" so that I have the opportunity to explain just how important these post-training meetings are and how to run them successfully. I have found that supervisors tend to react positively to my "selling" efforts if they are convinced that the work unit (and they themselves) will benefit.

PRE/POST ASSESSMENT TECHNIQUE

Purpose
The purpose of this technique is to compare trainees' assessments of how much impact the training program has had on their competence.

Description
1. Provide each trainee with a set of blank rating scales for each competency, indicating only the "high" and "low" levels of the scale. For example:
2. Ask each trainee to place an "x" on the scale to indicate their proficiency before the course and an "o" to indicate their proficiency after the course. For example:

Accuracy: low _____ x _____ o _____ high

3. It can be useful to ask the supervisor and/or manager to rate the trainee, in the same manner, after he/she has been back on the job for several weeks..

Strengths and Weaknesses
Pre/Post Assessment is a very simple and useful technique for obtaining self-report data concerning comparative competency before and after the training program. Although this technique yields highly subjective data, it is a good way of getting trainees and their supervisors to think in terms of performance improvement. Consequently the technique has both evaluative and educational payoffs. The lack of "absolute" accuracy inherent in such a technique is offset by the fact that it does obtain an interesting relative "guestimate" of comparative competence.

Example

This technique was suggested to me by a trainer with the Canadian government. He has found this technique to be extremely useful as a method of assessing changes due to training. He uses Pre/Post Assessment with both trainees and supervisors. From using the technique, he is able to obtain what he believes is an acceptable reading of the effectiveness of the training program on various performance-based dimensions. "It may not be perfect," he told me, "but it is much better than most of the evaluation techniques that are being used today!" In the light of the confusion surrounding the evaluation of training, this pragmatic statement is particularly believable.

DELAYED QUESTIONNAIRE TECHNIQUE

Purpose

Delayed Questionnaires are not late! They are purposely delayed to obtain feedback from trainees concerning their impressions of the course, when that they have had some opportunity to apply what they learned on the job.

Description

1. Design a questionnaire (see Figure 20) that asks trainees about their experiences in using their new knowledge and skills on the job.
2. Send out this Delayed Questionnaire approximately three weeks after the course to all trainees.
3. Follow-up with a friendly telephone call if you do not receive the questionnaire back within one week.

Strengths and Weaknesses

Delayed Questionnaires are often quite effective at obtaining information from trainees about the extent to which their training is paying off for them on the job. After all, this is the "bottom line" for training. Unfortunately, questionnaires (and especially follow-up questionnaires) are notorious for their high rates of *nonreturn*. Once trainees return to the job, they have a new set of

```
┌─────────────────────────────────────────────────────────┐
│              FOLLOW-UP QUESTIONNAIRE                     │
│ Course: _____        │
│ Name: _____ Date: _____         │
│                                                          │
│   On the basis of your past two weeks' experience back on the job,
│ please place a check-mark on each scale below, indicating your impres-
│ sions of the course.
│   Thanks for your help!
│
│  Immediately    ┌─┬─┬─┬─┬─┬─┬─┐   Not
│  applicable     └─┴─┴─┴─┴─┴─┴─┘   applicable
│  on the job
│
│  Well           ┌─┬─┬─┬─┬─┬─┬─┐
│  organized      └─┴─┴─┴─┴─┴─┴─┘   Disorganized
│
│  Interesting    ┌─┬─┬─┬─┬─┬─┬─┐   Dull
│                 └─┴─┴─┴─┴─┴─┴─┘
└─────────────────────────────────────────────────────────┘
```

Figure 20. Delayed Questionnaire.

---

priorities. However, a friendly telephone call may well overcome inertia.

Example

One training colleague of mine who works for an airline swears by his approach to the Delayed Questionnaire (while others swear at it!). He obtains almost a 100 percent return by doing the following:

    1. Keeping the questionnaire to one page.
    2. Testing the questionnaire for clarity before sending it out.
    3. Providing clear and unambiguous instructions.
    4. Making the questionnaire attractive.
    5. Sending a "personal" form-letter with a friendly tone, thanking trainees for their participation in the course.

Evaluation of Learning

   6. Including a self-addressed, stamped envelope.

ACTION PLAN FOLLOW-UP TECHNIQUE

Purpose
Let's not forget those Action Plans that we said were so very important. We can't just drop them. This technique provides a mechanism for reinforcing the importance of following-through on those commitments and for obtaining useful evaluation data.

Description
1. Brief supervisors on the importance of following-up with their subordinates on Action Plans produced during training courses.
2. Contact supervisors after the course to ensure that meetings have been scheduled with trainees to discuss their Action Plans.
3. Contact supervisors after the scheduled meeting to obtain feedback. Find out the extent to which:
   a. Action Plan commitments were realistic.
   b. Trainees are following-through on their Action Plan commitments.
   c. The training program was relevant to the on-the-job performance requirements of the trainee.
4. Contact the trainee to discuss the success of their meeting with the supervisor and other post-course comments.

Strengths and Weaknesses
Action Plan Follow-up is an extremely important post-course evaluation activity. It provides another opportunity to stay in contact with the trainees and their supervisors and to encourage them to follow-through on commitments made before and during the training course. However, unless you have solid relationships with supervisors, and they are convinced of the importance of post-training follow-up, this may be a frustrating activity. Many trainers learn at this time just how little supervisory support they have. It is remarkable how soon people forget the commitments that they made earlier to you and to each other in good faith.

Example

One telephone company training manager has done such a good job of educating supervisors that she receives tremendous cooperation from them in following-up on trainee action plans. For a long time, she either personally called or visited all trainess after the course to discuss their action plans. These regular sessions helped build trust and created an excellent example for supervisors. It is hard for trainers to have much credibility if they are not willing to do the same work they expect of supervisors. Now, all this work seems to have paid off. But this success has not come easily. Recently she confided in me that what I was now observing was the result of five years of laying the groundwork. In this lies an extremely important lesson for all of us. Training is hard work, but ensuring follow-up after training is even harder. The soil must be prepared for planting by nurturing relationships with managers and supervisors. A training department that is isolated from the job is a training department that cannot expect much on-the-job performance improvement. The extent of the cooperation that you receive in implementing such follow-up techniques as this one is a good indicator of how well you have "laid the groundwork."

EVALUATION INTERVIEW TECHNIQUE

Purpose

The Evaluation Interview is a post-training evaluation technique that can provide a great deal of valuable information about the effects of training. It can also be useful as a method of reminding trainees of their responsibilities for using what they learned in their job.

Description

1. Make an appointment with each trainee approximately three weeks after the end of the course.
2. Ask trainess questions concerning the following:
    a. What they learned in the course that was most useful to them on the job.

Evaluation of Learning

  b. What they learned in the course that was least helpful to them on the job.
  c. Problems they have encountered in trying to use their new knowledge and skills on the job.
  d. What they would have liked the course to have covered.
  e. Suggestions for future improvements in the course.
3. It is useful to take this opportunity to review trainee Action Plans and other commitments to action that were made during the training program.
4. Give whatever "moral support" you can. Suggest another meeting at a later date if you feel it might be useful.
5. If in-person interviews are impossible, the Evaluation Interview can be done by telephone.

Strengths and Weaknesses

Interviews can be extremely powerful information gathering techniques, since they allow highly personal and focused discussions. They also allow for probing follow-up questions. The Evaluation Interview is useful as an opportunity to reinforce course content and commitments, as well as for acquiring evaluation data.

However, one should recognize that all interviews require considerable time investment and questioning skills, as well as a substantial commitment on the part of both trainee and trainer. If this commitment is lacking, the technique will probably not be successful. Obviously, Evaluation Interviews will be difficult if there is substantial geographical distance separating the trainees from the trainer. However, as mentioned above, Evaluation Interviews can be done by telephone.

Example

One Fortune 500 company with which I worked as a consultant uses the Evaluation Interview widely in its post-training evaluation. Trainers take turns running the interviews. The Training Manager believes that doing the interviews puts his training staff in closer contact with the workplace, highlights their visibility (no ivory tower prima donnas these trainers), and emphasizes the importance that is placed on training and evaluation. Due to the large number of employees trained, they randomly select trainees for interviews. While this reduces the time it takes to complete the interviews, the random selection still ensures that the information collected is valid. Corporate trainers report that they learn a tremendous amount from these interviews and that the Evaluation Interview technique enables them to acquire a depth and quality of data that could not be collected by questionnaires alone.

CRITICAL INCIDENT EVALUATION TECHNIQUE

Purpose

The purpose of the Critical Incident Evaluation technique is to collect anecdotal information concerning the results of the training program on job performance. This technique acquires a very high quality of performance-based data that is useful for summative evaluation as well as for training program redesign.

Description

1. Contact the supervisors of employees who have recently attended a training course.
2. Ask supervisors to identify "incidents" in trainees' work performance that might indicate that training has or has not been successful.
3. Provide supervisors with examples of the types of "incidents" that they should be looking for. You might provide supervisors with a "critical incident" checklist, so that they might be able to check-off incidents as they occur. See Figure 21.
4. You might also ask trainees to record "incidents" that they have noticed in their own performance.

Strengths and Weaknesses

The Critical Incident Evaluation technique can provide very useful, performance-based evaluation information. Unfortunately, it is a rather difficult technique to use effectively, and it requires an exceptional amount of cooperation on the part of supervisors. The difficulty derives from the fact that, in using this technique, supervisors must *observe* and *record* subordinate behaviors "in real time," or soon after they occur. This is quite a lot to expect.

Evaluation of Learning

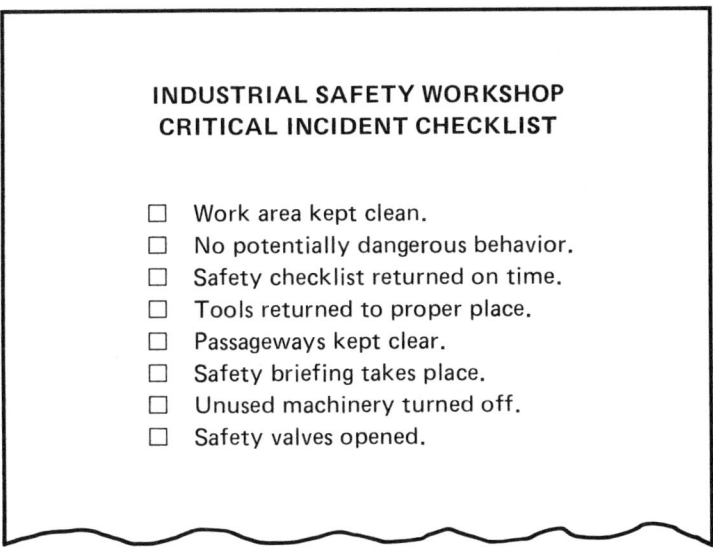

Figure 21. Critical Incident Checklist.

However, the Critical Incident Evaluation technique can be limited to a set block of time (say, one day), thus reducing the magnitude of the supervisor's time commitment.

Example

In one state government agency, the Critical Incident Evaluation technique is working very effectively. In this case, participating supervisors have been trained in how to identify and record critical incidents, and they do so very competently. Most supervisors have attended a supervisory training course that has presented a variation on the "critical incident" technique used for employee performance appraisal. Adapting the technique to course evaluation was a very small step for these supervisors, who did not need to learn the technique from scratch. Tasks being observed were somewhat repetitive, and the Critical Incident Evaluation technique was able to identify key behaviors that had not changed adequately as a result of training. This feedback proved extremely valuable for course redesign. On the positive side, it also identified where training had been successful. Supervisor's "critical incident" journals continue to be a central and rich source of training evaluation information.

ASK THE CLASS TECHNIQUE

Purpose
Ask the Class is exactly what it sounds like, a straightforward attempt to discover class attitudes toward the training experience. The purpose of this technique is to get individual qualitative responses to questions at the end of a training program.

Description
1. Ask the Class a series of questions concerning the impact, strengths, and weaknesses of the course. This should be done at the end of the final class session. Responses should be recorded and compared with other evaluative measures.
2. Questions could include the following:
    a. What was your reaction to the program?
    b. What did you like most about the program?
    c. What did you like least about the program?
    d. What did you learn that you feel will be easiest to implement back on the job?
    e. What did you learn that you feel will be most difficult to implement back on the job?
    f. How supportive do you feel your supervisor will be when you try to use your new skills and knowledge back on the job?
    g. Can you name specific ways *your* performance will improve as a result of this program?
3. This technique can be used in a class context or it can be the basis of a series of individual interviews at a later time.

Strengths and Weaknesses
Ask the Class is a simple and straightforward technique for dis-

covering trainee attitudes toward a training program. It does not require any instrumentation and needs little planning. It also has the advantage of a refreshing informality. Essentially, you are saying: "Let's have a little chat on what you thought about the program." This is much less intimidating than a formal survey. It is also likely to obtain more interesting feedback than could be obtained from a paper-and-pencil instrument.

On the negative side of the ledger, there may be a resistance to share views publicly. There is sometimes a reluctance to criticize openly. However, its trainers have been successful in developing rapport with trainees during the program, this should not be the case. The openness with which trainees share during an Ask the Class session may be a useful indicator of the degree of trust that was developed during the program. Another possible problem might be the unwillingness of some to share, while the more vociferous members of the class might be dominant. This will not always give a legitimate view of trainee reactions. However, regardless of the nature of the feedback, it will enhance your evaluative data base, especially when analyzed in concert with other data sources.

Example

A senior trainer for a large transportation company uses Ask the Class at the end of virtually every program. He does not believe in the traditional "happiness index," but he does like to receive some immediate feedback. This outstanding trainer is convinced that the best immediate feedback on trainee reaction can be obtained through more informal lines of communication. He asks just a few direct questions (such as those suggested above). He receives some good, honest answers, but more "gut" reactions than well thought-out evaluations. Not a strong believer in quick-response instruments, he sends out a delayed questionnaire asking for more detailed responses, at a time when he believes trainees are in a better position to elaborate.

MATERIALS REVIEW TECHNIQUE

Purpose
The purpose of Materials Review is to better understand the learning process that occurred (or didn't occur) during the training program. It is also very useful to helping trainers realize the uniquenesses of individuals and their personal learning styles.

Description
1. At the beginning of the program, tell trainees that one way you intend to evaluate the program is to look at their course materials, including their notes and how they marked up their materials.
2. At the end (or toward the end) of the program, ask trainees to hand in their course materials, so that you can review them.
3. Carefully review the materials for notations, pictures, diagrams, marginal comments, note-taking, etc.
4. Return the materials to trainees as promptly as possible with a note of thanks.

Strengths and Weaknesses
Materials Review is an excellent way to see how trainees are learning. Trainee notations, diagrams, doodles, etc., are often very revealing. This process can also indicate where there are questions and when active learning may not be taking place. In most cases, active learning will be physically apparent in most trainees' notebooks and course materials. Materials review could also provide the stimulus to teach trainees how to process course material more actively. It is striking how much one can tell about the learning process by reviewing trainees' course materials!

There are few weaknesses of this technique, as long as the proper trusting atmosphere is developed. I do not think that trainees would be reluctant to show off their course materials, as long as they feel the information (some of it very personal) will be held in strict confidence. One other consideration is that you may be depriving trainees of these materials when they need them on the job. That is why the prompt return of the materials is important. Materials review can be accomplished in an evening. This will eliminate the time problem.

Evaluation of Learning

Example

A trainer for a large electronics firm first suggested Materials Review to me as a discrete evaluation tool. I had previously been using this technique informally. For instance, when I was talking to a trainee about a course, I would look in his or her notebook as we discussed certain points. I would often see interesting diagrams and graphic depictions of points raised, but I never thought of reviewing this material systematically. My colleague, however, has done this regularly for several years. He asks for trainees to hand in their manuals and course notes for one day, just enough time to review them. This creative trainer insists that this technique has provided him with a vast array of new methods for presenting instructional content.

Once I started using Materials Review more systematically, I found that the same thing happened. Many trainees were extremely creative in the manner in which they organized the subject matter. And, since they were closer to the work being done, their presentations turned out to be more job-relevant than mine! Materials review has significantly improved my practical knowledge and presentation skills by focusing my attention on ways trainees are likely to structure learning materials for on-the-job application.

Bibliography

Adler, M.J., *How to Speak, How to Listen.* New York: Macmillan, 1983.
Barzakov, I., *Optimalearning.* Mill Valley, CA: Barzakov Educational Foundation, 1985.
deBono, E., *Lateral Thinking.* New York: Harper, 1973.
Bramson, R.M., *Coping with Difficult People.* New York: Doubldeay, 1981.
Broadwell, M.M., *The Supervisor as an Instructor.* Reading, MA: Addison-Wesley, 1978.
Broadwell, M.M., *The Supervisor and On-the-Job Training.* Reading, MA: Addison-Wesley, 1975.
Buzan, T., *Use Both Sides of Your Brain.* New York: Dutton, 1975.
Buzan, T., *Make the Most of Your Mind.* New York: Simon and Schuster, 1977.
Carnevale, A.P., and Goldstein, H., *Employee Training.* Washington, D.C.: ASTD, 1983.
Craig, R.L. (Ed.), *Training and Development Handbook.* New York: McGraw-Hill, 1976.
Davies, I.K., *Instructional Technique.* New York: McGraw-Hill, 1981.
Donaldson, L., and Scannel, E.E., *Human Resource Development.* Reading, MA: Addison-Wesley, 1978.
Ericksen, S.C., *Motivation for Learning.* Ann Arbor: University of Michigan, 1974.
Gagne, R.M., and Briggs, L.J., *Principles of Instructional Design.* New York: Holt, Rinehart, & Winston, 1974.
Glaser, R. (Ed.), *The Nature of Reinforcement.* New York: Academic Press, 1971.
Gilbert, T.F., *Human Competence.* New York: McGraw-Hill, 1978.
Goldstein, A.P., and Sorcher, M., *Changing Supervisor Behavior.* New York: Pergamon, 1974.
Hall, J., *The Competence Process.* Woodlands, TX: Teleometrics, 1980.
Hamblin, A.C., *Evaluation and Control of Training.* London: McGraw-Hill, 1974.
Heinich, R., Molenda, M., and Russell, J.D., *Instructional Media* (Second Edition). New York: John Wiley, 1985.
Knowles, M.C., *Self-Directed Learning.* Chicago: Follett, 1975.
Laird, D., and House, R., *Training Today's Employees.* Boston: CBI, 1983.
Mager, R., *Preparing Instructional Objectives.* Belmont, CA: Fearon, 1975.

Melton, R.F., *Instructional Models for Course Design and Development.* Englewood Cliffs, NJ: Educational Technology Publications, 1984.

Norman, D.A., *Memory and Attention: An Introduction to Information Processing.* New York: John Wiley, 1969.

Osborne, A.F., *Applied Imagination.* New York: Scribner's, 1979.

Ribler, R.I., *Training Development Guide.* Reston, VA: Reston Publishing, 1983.

Russell, P., *The Brain Book.* New York: New American, 1979.

Sanders, D.A., and Sanders, J.A., *Teaching Creativity Through Metaphor.* New York: Longman, 1984.

Smith, Robert M., *Learning How to Learn.* Chicago: Follett, 1982.

Travers, R.M.W., *Essentials of Learning.* New York: Macmillan, 1977.

Trow, W.C., and Hadden, E.E. (Eds.), *Psychological Foundations of Educational Technology.* Englewood Cliffs, NJ: Educational Technology Publications, 1976.

Warrick, D.D., and Zawacki, R.A., *Supervisory Management.* New York: Harper & Row, 1984.

Index

Acknowledging Feelings Technique, 30
Action Plan Follow-Up Technique, 131
Action Planning Technique, 108
Ask the Class Technique, 136
Associative Thinking Technique, 62

Barzakov, I., 33, 69
Before and After Technique, 120
Benefits and Costs Technique, 122
Bibliography, 141
Brainstorming, 86-87
Bumper Stickers Technique, 87

Card Sorting Technique, 124
Case Studies Technique, 82
Categorization of Notes Technique, 73
Cleese, J., 55
Competency Visioning Technique, 36
Concept Diagramming Technique, 65
Concept Examples Technique, 63
Concert Reading Technique, 69
Course Agreement, 24
Creative Name Tags Technique, 31
Critical Incident Evaluation Technique, 134

Delayed Questionnaire Technique, 129
Developing Analogies Technique, 89
Drill Practice Technique, 53

Environmental Enrichment Technique, 32
Evaluation Indicator Identification Technique, 118
Evaluation Interview Technique, 132
Evaluation of Learning, 111

Feedback Cards Technique, 111
Fill in the Blanks Technique, 71
Flip-Chart Feedback Technique, 113

Gilbert, T.F., 44
Glossary Development Technique, 75
Group Learning, 3
Groups, 3
Guided Imagery Technique, 98

Happiness Index Technique, 115
Human Competence, 44
Humor Technique, 54

Individual Brainstorming Technique, 86
Individuals, 3-5
Inviting Recall Technique, 59

Key Concept Recording Technique, 60

Learning, 6-9
Lozanov, G., 33

Materials Review Technique, 138

143

Media, 50
Memory, 7
Metaphor Technique, 67
Mock Interview Technique, 52
Multi-Method Presentation Technique, 49
Multi-Phase Programming Technique, 78

Note-Taking Technique, 85

Objective Review Technique, 74
Objective Rewriting Technique, 90
Organizing Information, 49
Overviewing Technique, 40

Perception, 7
Periodic Summarizing Technique, 68
Personal Learning Journal Technique, 96
Personal Needs Analysis Technique, 33
Personal Objective Review Technique, 46
Personal Performance Analysis Technique, 44
Personal Vantage Point Technique, 58
Potential Problem Analysis Technique, 103
Practice for Retrieval, 78
Pre-Course Action Planning Technique, 42
Pre-Course Contract Technique, 22
Pre-Course Trainee-Supervisor Discussions Technique, 14
Pre-Course Trainee-Trainer Contacts Technique, 16
Preliminary Exercises Technique, 20

Pre/Post Assessment Technique, 128
Problem-Solving, 100-101
Problem-Solving Technique, 100
Problems into Opportunities Technique, 105
Programmed Instruction, 72

Quality Circles, 101
Quality Dot Technique, 101
Question Recording Technique, 56
Quizzing Technique, 114

Relaxation, 27-30, 98
Relaxation 1: Deep Breathing Technique, 27
Relaxation 2: Progressive Relaxation Technique, 28
Repetition Technique, 70

Scavenger Hunt Technique, 95
Self-Affirmation Technique, 38
Shoulds, Wants, Wills Technique, 91
Simulation Technique, 84
Suggestology, 33
Superlearning, 69
Supervisor, 10, 15, 22, 25-26, 80, 82, 126-127
Supervisor Briefings Technique, 25
Supervisor Meetings Technique, 80

Trainee-Developed Evaluation Technique, 117
Trainee-Supervisor Evaluation Meeting Technique, 126
Trainee Teaching Technique, 94
Training Needs Questionnaire Technique, 18

Video Feedback Technique, 107
Videotape, 50, 107